creating
a web site in
dreamweaver cs4

Visual QuickProject Guide

by Nolan Hester

Peachpit
Press

Visual QuickProject Guide
Creating a Web Site in Dreamweaver CS4
Nolan Hester

Peachpit Press

1249 Eighth Street
Berkeley, CA 94710
510/524-2178
510/524-2221 (fax)

Find us on the Web at: www.peachpit.com
To report errors, please send a note to errata@peachpit.com
Peachpit Press is a division of Pearson Education

Editor: Nancy Davis
Production Editor: David Van Ness
Compositor: David Van Ness
Proofreader: Tracy D. O'Connell
Indexer: FireCrystal Communications
Cover design: Peachpit Press, Aren Howell
Interior design: Elizabeth Castro
Cover photo credit: Daniel Loiselle

ISBN 13: 978-0-321-59150-0
ISBN 10:   0-321-59150-X

9 8 7 6 5 4 3 2 1

Printed and bound in the United States of America

This one remains
dedicated to Mom.

Special Thanks to...

Nancy Davis, my editor, for making my books way better over the past 10 years,

David Van Ness for being such a pro and a rock through more than 20 books,

Emily Glossbrenner of FireCrystal for always making every index a map of concepts rather than just a vocabulary list,

And, as always, Mary.

contents

introduction   vii

what you'll create	viii	useful tools	xiii
how this book works	x	the next step	xiv
the web site	xii		

1. welcome to dreamweaver   1

explore dreamweaver	2	extra bits	10
set up local site	8		

2. create a basic web site   11

create a home page	12	create lists	21
add text	15	add a footer	23
insert image placeholder	17	extra bits	24
create headings	19		

3. add images   25

image tools	26	adjust brightness	36
add image	27	create thumbnail image	37
add flash video	29	replace placeholder	40
add quicktime video	32	flow text around images	42
crop image	34	extra bits	44

4. add tables   45

add a table	46	sort tables	55
select, change table parts	48	extra bits	57
import tabular data	52		

contents

5. create links   59

link text internally	60	link image	66
link text externally	62	create image map	67
add email link	63	color site links	70
add anchor link	64	extra bits	75

6. use style sheets   77

using the css styles tab	78	create a compound style	86
using the properties panel	80	create class-based style	93
detach, attach style sheets	82	extra bits	96
create a tag-based style	84		

7. add interactivity   97

add navigation menu	98	create form	106
add jump menu	103	extra bits	112

8. reuse items to save time   113

create a favorite	114	edit library item	118
use a favorite	115	insert library item	119
create a library item	116	extra bits	120

9. publish site   121

add search terms	122	connect to remote site	129
check and fix links	124	upload multiple files	130
explore the files panel	125	upload a single page	132
set up remote site	127	extra bits	133

index   135

introduction

The Visual QuickProject Guide that you hold in your hands offers a unique way to learn about new technologies. Instead of drowning you in theoretical possibilities and lengthy explanations, this Visual QuickProject Guide uses big, color illustrations coupled with clear, concise step-by-step instructions to show you how to complete one specific project in a matter of hours.

Our project in this book is to create a beautiful Web site using Adobe Dreamweaver CS4, one of the best programs for building Web sites. Our Web site describes the tours and services of a fictitious travel agency. Because the project covers all the techniques needed to build a basic Web site, you'll be able to use what you learn to create your own Web site. Thanks to Dreamweaver, you'll do all this without having to enter a single line of HTML, the code that drives the Web.

You can use the book two ways. Download the examples at the companion Web site and literally follow each step, chapter by chapter. Or you can create your own site and use the steps as a general guide as you build the items explained in each section and chapter. OK, there's a third way: Use the examples to get your feet wet, and then plunge into building your totally cool site based on what you learn here. Any way you approach it, it'll be fun.

what you'll create

Besides the usual text, headings, and tables, here are some of the things you'll learn to create with Dreamweaver.

Use Cascading Style Sheets to generate clean layouts with site-wide headers, sidebars, and main content areas. (See page 12 and Chapter 6 on page 77.)

Add a variety of images, plus Flash and QuickTime videos, to give pages visual punch. (See pages 27, 29 and 32.)

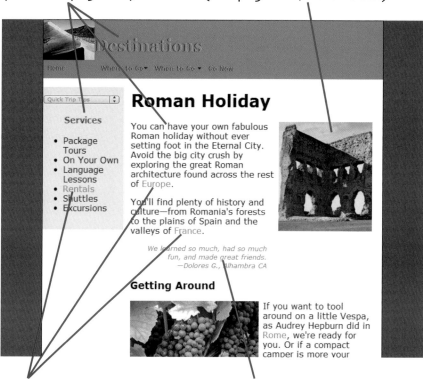

Add internal, external, and email links, then give them a consistent appearance using style sheets. (See Chapter 5 on page 59.)

Create special formats that can be applied to any item, such as pull quotes, and quickly update them anytime. (See page 93.)

Add a jump menu to give visitors a quick view of other items on your site. (See page 103.)

Create an interactive navigation menu to guide visitors as they explore your site. (See page 98.)

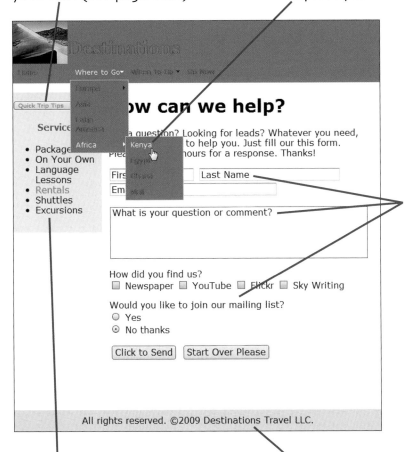

Design easy-to-use forms for collecting information from visitors. (See page 106.)

Quickly create item lists and style them just as quickly. (See page 21.)

Create library items with a consistent look for repeated use across your site. (See page 116.)

how this book works

The title explains what is covered in that section.

Names of Dreamweaver elements, file names, and other important concepts are shown in orange.

create thumbnail image

If you have an image without lots of details, you can use it to create a tiny thumbnail to add some graphic variety to a page. Detail lost from reducing and resampling cannot be recovered, so use a duplicate of your original image. (See extra bits on page 44.)

Numbered steps lead you through the sequence of actions, showing only the details you really need.

1 Click in the page where you want to use the duplicate of your original image (Copy of dune300.jpg in our example in a blank duplicate we created of the index page named dunepage.html). Choose Image from the Image button's drop-down menu to insert the image (or drag the image directly to the page from its listing in the Files tab).

2 Click to select the image, then press Shift as you drag one of the image's corner handles. This reduces the image while maintaining its proportions.

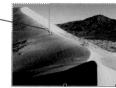

Watch the pixel dimensions change in the W and H text windows in the Properties panel to gauge how much to reduce the image. (In our example, we want reduce the image to a width of 100 pixels.)

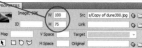

Screenshots focus on what part of Dreamweaver you'll be using for that particular project step.

3 Release the cursor and the image appears with the new dimensions in bold—even though the actual size of the file remains the same. The circling arrow connecting the two numbers is meant to remind you of what comes next.

add images   37

The extra bits section at the end of each chapter contains additional tips and tricks that you might like to know—but that aren't absolutely necessary for creating the Web page. As you work through a section, flip back to see the related extra bits rather than wait until you finish the entire chapter.

crop image

extra bits

image tools p. 26
- Ignore the blank ID text window to the right of the Properties panel's thumbnail image, which is for scripts.

add image p. 27
- The root folder contains all your Web site's files. (In our example, it's DWcs4_ExampleSite.) An images subfolder within the root folder makes it easier to find your photos or graphics.
- Always add Alt text for your images. Special audio Web browsers also use Alt text for visually impaired visitors. If the image is something like a horizontal rule, choose <empty> from the drop-down menu.

add flash video p. 29
- In step 4, if the swf or flv file already is in your site folder, you can click and drag it from the Files tab directly onto the page.
- In step 7, when Dreamweaver adds the swf scripts, it also displays the related JavaScript file in the Related Files toolbar just below the tab for your video page.

crop image p. 34
- In our example, we crop an image already inserted into a page. You also can open an image directly from the Files panel, make your crops, and then insert it into a page. Choose the workflow that feels most natural, then stick with it for consistent results.
- It's easy to wind up with several different sizes of the same image for different sections of your layout. By including the image's pixel width at the end of its name, such as janustemple180.jpg, it's easy to remember which is which.

adjust brightness p. 36
- The sliders can be hard to control, so type numbers in the text windows for fine adjustments.

create thumbnail image p. 37
- You could use resampling to enlarge an image, but don't. The quality will suffer noticeably. Instead, use your regular image-editing program with the (presumably) larger original.
- When you click the Resample button, a dialog warns you that the change is permanent. Since we're using a duplicate, click OK.

44   add images

The heading for each group of tips matches the section title. (The colors are just for decoration and have no hidden meaning.)

Next to the heading there's a page number that also shows which section the tips belong to.

the web site

You can find this book's companion site at
http://www.waywest.net/dwvqj/.

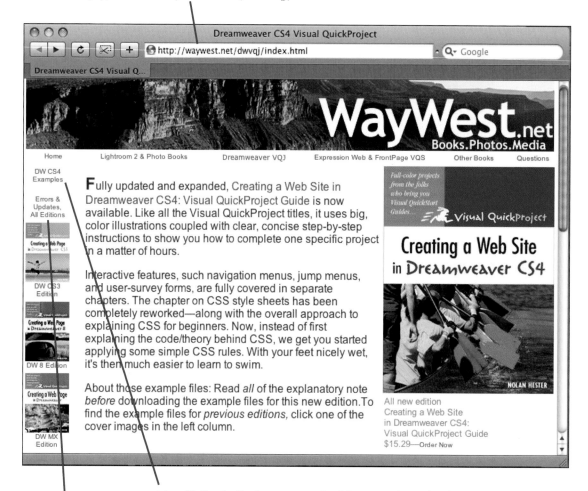

You'll find all the example files used in the book,
including the images, along with detailed instructions
on how to use them as you work through the book.

You'll also find extra tips on working with Dreamweaver,
plus corrections if any mistakes are found.

useful tools

Naturally, you'll need a computer and Dreamweaver CS4, which is packed with most of the tools you'll need, including a way to publish to the Web.

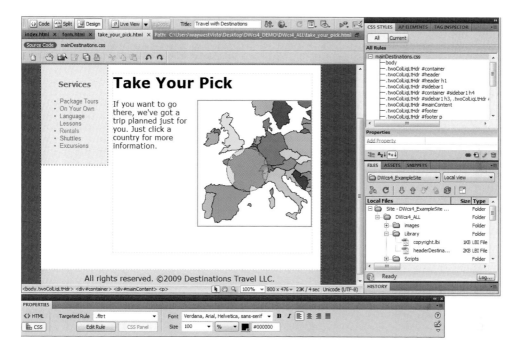

You'll also need an image editor. If you bought Dreamweaver as part of the Adobe Creative Suite 4 Web Standard or Web Premium editions, then you'll be able to use Fireworks. The Web Premium edition also includes Photoshop. Both programs are designed to work hand-in-hand with Dreamweaver. Your digital camera may have included an image-editing program. Otherwise, consider Adobe Photoshop Elements, which also contains specific tools for working with Web images.

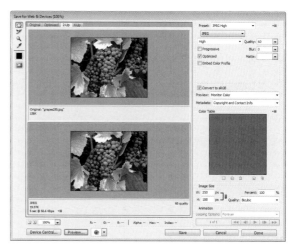

the next step

While this Visual QuickProject Guide gives you a good start on creating a Web site using Dreamweaver, there is a lot more to learn. If you want to dive into all the details, try Dreamweaver CS4 for Windows and Macintosh: Visual QuickStart Guide, by Tom Negrino and Dori Smith.

The Dreamweaver CS4: Visual Quick-Start Guide features clear examples, concise step-by-step instructions, and tons of helpful tips. With more than 550 pages, it covers darn near every aspect of Dreamweaver.

VISUAL QUICKSTART GUIDE

DREAMWEAVER CS4

Learn Dreamweaver CS4 the Quick and Easy Way!

FOR WINDOWS AND MACINTOSH

TOM NEGRINO DORI SMITH

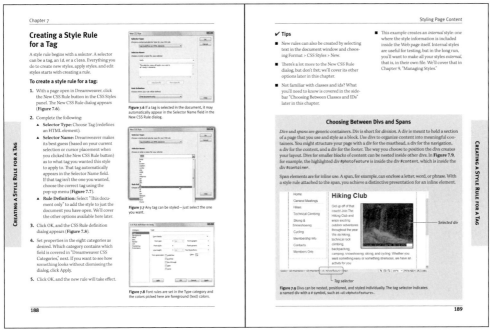

1. welcome to dreamweaver

Adobe Dreamweaver CS4 is a powerful program, packed with cool features to create Web sites. So packed, in fact, that it can be a bit overwhelming.

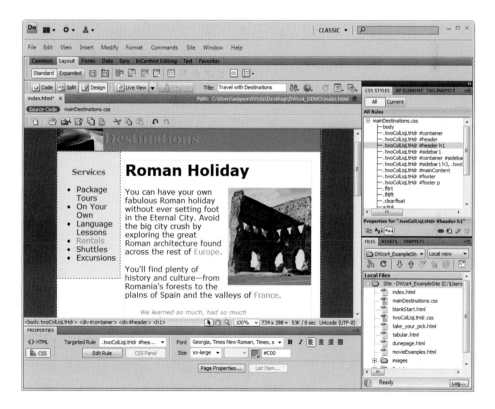

Not to worry. We aren't going to explain every possible option—just the crucial ones to keep you going, no matter how daunting Dreamweaver may seem initially. We'll have some fun along the way, too, so let's get started.

explore dreamweaver

A series of key toolbars, windows, and panels surrounds your main Dreamweaver document. Take a moment to understand how these tools work and you'll save yourself frustration later.

By default, the Document toolbar is set to the Design view. You can change it to show only the Code view or use the Split view to show the Code and Design views. You now can change the horizontal split by choosing View > Split Vertically.

The new Live View button enables you to see some effects, such as a movie embedded in a page, without using your Web browser. (See the first "explore dreamweaver" extra bit on page 10.)

The current file's title appears at the center of the toolbar, followed by some buttons related to posting your site on the Web.

Use the high-lighted button to see a ruler or grid while building pages.

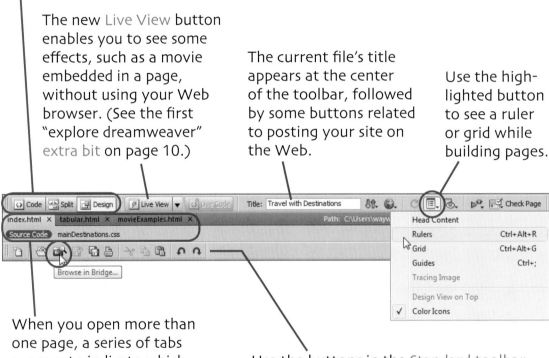

When you open more than one page, a series of tabs appears to indicate which ones are open. Files related to the open pages, such as supporting CSS or JavaScript coding, can be viewed by clicking their names just below the tabs.

Use the buttons in the Standard toolbar to create new files, open folders, cut and paste, save files, and undo actions. The highlighted button enables you to switch to Adobe Bridge, a great tool included with Dreamweaver for quickly finding images on your computer that lie outside your Web site folder. (See the second "explore dreamweaver" extra bit on page 10.)

Choose Window > Insert to show the Insert toolbar/panel. The Common tab and the other tabs display related buttons for a variety of tasks. To show or hide toolbars, choose View > Toolbars and make a choice in the drop-down menu. (To expand or collapse the Insert toolbar, click the arrow next to Insert.)

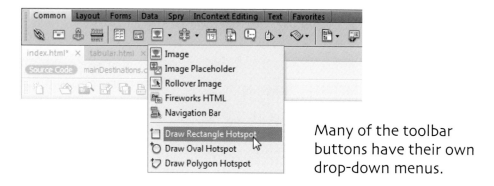

Many of the toolbar buttons have their own drop-down menus.

The Layout tab includes four buttons for creating dynamic items such as drop-down menus, tabbed panels, and mouse-triggered expansion or collapse of page sections. While based on JavaScript, these Spry widgets are easy to use, making quick work of adding navigation menus to your Web pages. (See page 98.)

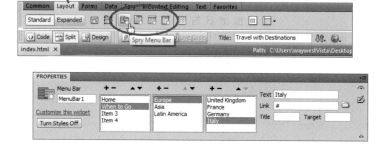

explore dreamweaver (cont.)

Depending on what you've selected, the Properties panel changes to display the relevant information and tools, such as those for text or images. By adding a CSS button to the panel, Dreamweaver now makes it clear when you are generating CSS code instead of HTML.

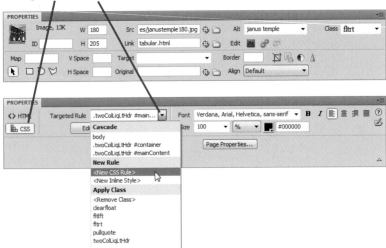

To see or hide the Properties panel, press Ctrl F3 (Windows) or ⌘ F3 (Mac).

As part of Adobe's efforts to make all of its CS4 applications work similarly, Dreamweaver now lets you choose how your windows and panels are arranged in what are called workspaces. The Classic workspace is used throughout this book, but you can use the drop-down menu to choose any of eight workspaces.

Or adjust an existing workspace to your liking and save it by chooosing New Workspace. (See the third "explore dreamweaver" extra bit on page 10.)

To collapse all the right-side panels into a compact panel of icons, click the double arrow in the top-right corner. Do the same to expand the icon panel back to full panels. (See the fourth "explore dreamweaver" extra bit on page 10.)

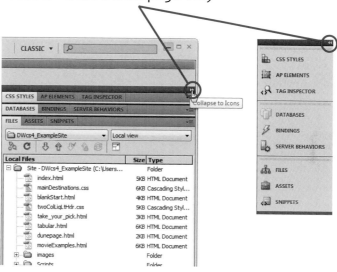

To expand a single panel, click its icon.

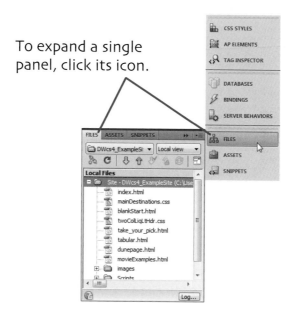

explore dreamweaver (cont.)

The Files panel group gives you quick access to all your site's files, plus Assets and Snippets, which show your most used images, color swatches, and bits of code.

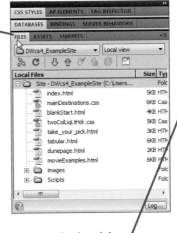

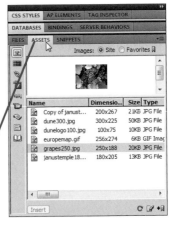

To collapse any panel, double-click its tab; double-click any tab in the collapsed panel stack to re-expand that panel.

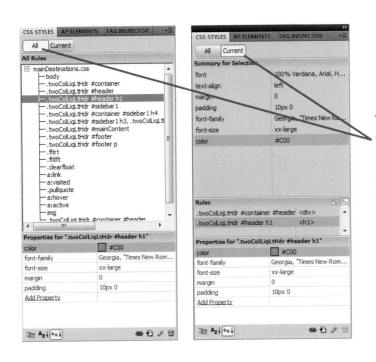

The CSS Styles tab helps you keep track of all styles used in a page (left) or the details of the currently selected style (right). For more details, see page 78.

Dreamweaver CS4 also comes with Adobe Bridge, a great program that helps you quickly find images even if they are scattered across many folders and multiple hard drives. You can launch the program directly or by clicking the Bridge button in Dreamweaver's Standard toolbar (see page 2).

Click Bridge's upper-right button to toggle between a compact and big-screen view of your image files.

The Favorites panel makes it easy to jump among your most used images. You can drag images directly from Bridge into Dreamweaver Web pages.

The Folders panel lets you navigate on your computer to find images.

Use the slider to zoom in or out on the thumbnails.

Click to switch among four view setups or create a custom view setup.

set up local site

Once you've installed Dreamweaver, your first step is to set up a local version of your Web site on your computer.

1 Launch Dreamweaver and when the Start Page appears, click the Dreamweaver Site button.

2 Dreamweaver automatically assigns a generic name to your new site and highlights it in the Basic tab of the Site Definition dialog box. Switch to the Advanced screen by clicking the tab.

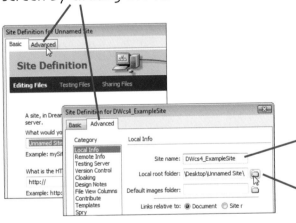

3 Replace the assigned name with a more descriptive name. (In our example, it's DWcs4_ExampleSite.) (See the first "set up local site" extra bit on page 10.)

4 Click the folder button to set the Local root folder where you'll store all the site's files on your computer.

welcome to dreamweaver

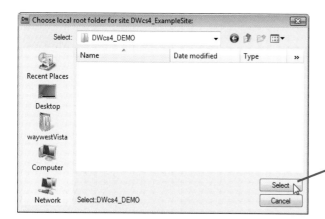

5 Navigate to where you want to store the local root folder, select or create a folder, and click Select (Windows) or Choose (Mac). (See the second "set up local site" extra bit on page 10.)

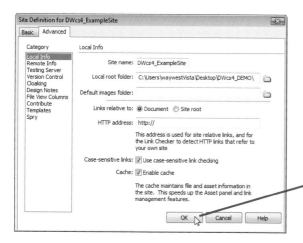

6 That's all we need to do for now, so when the Site Definition dialog box reappears, click OK to close the dialog box.

7 The local site is added to the Files panel. You're ready to start building your site, as explained in the next chapter.

extra bits

explore dreamweaver p. 2

- Unless you're familiar with HTML or CSS coding, leave the toolbar set to Design.

- Rather than explain every tool and button here, we'll cover them in the coming chapters as we need them. We also don't cover items more suited to experienced users, such as the Files panel's Snippets tab, which can store frequently used bits of code.

- The ability to switch workspaces is particularly handy if you sometimes use a laptop and other times a roomy desktop monitor.

- Switching Dreamweaver's panels to the compact icon setup solves the crowded-windows problem that previously frustrated laptop users.

set up local site p. 8

- The name you enter in the Site Definition window only appears within Dreamweaver, not on your actual Web site. Pick one to distinguish this site from the many others you'll no doubt be creating soon.

- If your computer has a second hard drive, store your root folder there instead of on your main hard drive. That way if the heavily used main drive goes bad, your local site files remain safe.

2. create a basic web site

Thanks to Dreamweaver's style sheet–based layouts, it's relatively simple to create a basic Web site with pages that share the same design and navigation buttons. In this chapter, you'll start by using a basic layout to create a simple home page. In later chapters, you'll learn to dress it up a bit with images and some special features. Here, however, we'll focus on the basics: creating, naming, titling, and saving this all-important page.

Our logo

Destinations

Services

- Package Tours
- On Your Own
- Language Lessons
- Rentals
- Shuttles
- Excursions

Roman Holiday

You can have your own fabulous Roman holididay without ever setting foot in the Eternal City. Avoid the big city crush by exploring the great Roman architecture found across the rest of Europe.

You'll find plenty of history and culture—from Romania's forests to the plains of Spain and the valleys of France.

Getting Around

If you want to tool around on a little Vespa, as Audrey Hepburn did in Rome, we're ready for you. Or if a compact camper is more your style, Gregory Peck just might want to go along.

All rights reserved. ©2007 Destinations Travel LLC.

Don't let this relatively plain example page fool you. Built with Dreamweaver's predesigned page layouts using Cascading Style Sheets, it offers a solid foundation for an entire Web site. Watch it grow as we move through each chapter.

create a home page

The mechanics of creating a home page for a Web site are pretty simple. The first step is to create a new page, then name the file, give it a title, and save it. While you can give the home page any title you wish (the title will appear at the top of the visitor's Web browser), use something that helps visitors immediately understand your site's purpose. If you have not already done so, launch Dreamweaver, and the site you defined in Chapter 1 opens by default.

1 Use the Menu bar to choose File > New (Ctrl N in Windows, ⌘N on the Mac).

2 When the New Document dialog box appears, select Blank Page on the left (HTML will be selected automatically in the middle) and then make a choice in the Layout column. In our example, we're using the two-column liquid layout with a left sidebar, header and footer. (Liquid simply means that the layout automatically adjusts to the width of the user's Web browser window—a good approach for most layouts.) (See the first "create a home page" extra bit on page 24.)

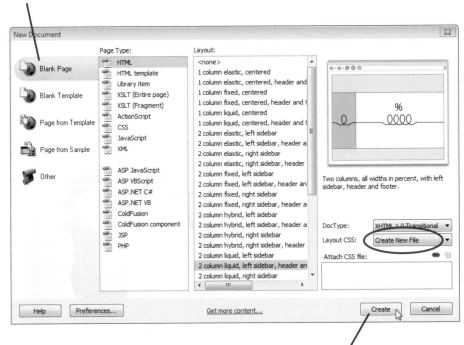

3 Below the right column's preview area, make sure the Layout CSS drop-down menu is set to Create New File before you click Create.

create a basic web site

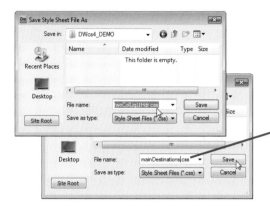

4 Dreamweaver automatically offers to save the site's style sheet in the root folder you defined in Chapter 1. But instead of applying a name based on the layout style (twoColLiqLtHdr.css in the example), name it based on your site's name (mainDestinations.css in the example). Click Save. (See the second "create a home page" extra bit on page 24.)

5 Dreamweaver saves the CSS page and adds it to the site's list of files. Its filename also appears in the Related Files toolbar just below the tab for the still untitled html file. You can click the style sheet's name (mainDestinations.css) whenever you want to see its coding.

6 Click inside the page's Title text window, and type in your own title for the page. (Our sample site uses Travel with Destinations, the name of our fictitious travel company.) Visitors to your site will see the title at the top of their browser window, where it acts as a label for your site. It's not the same as the page's file name—as you'll see in the next step.

create a home page (cont.)

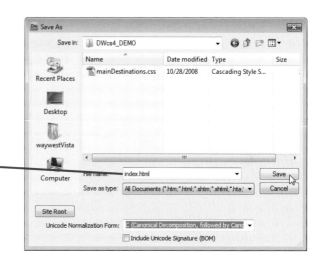

7 From the Menu bar, choose File > Save (Ctrl S in Windows, ⌘ S on the Mac). In the Save As dialog box that opens, navigate to the site folder you created in Chapter 1. This will be your home page, so name it index and click Save. (Dreamweaver automatically adds the .html suffix.) (See the third "create a home page" extra bit on page 24.)

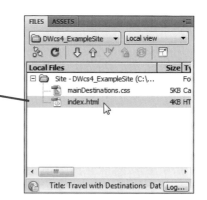

8 The page's name is added to the list of site files in the Files tab. Before going on, save your work (Ctrl S in Windows, ⌘ S on the Mac).

add text

Adding text to a Web page in Dreamweaver is not that different from using a word processing program, with the exception of using certain special characters explained in step 3. (See extra bits on page 24.)

1 Start by replacing some of the home page's placeholder material. Double-click the top header to select it, and type in your site's name. In our example, it's Destinations. Don't worry about how it looks— we'll format all this material later using style sheets.

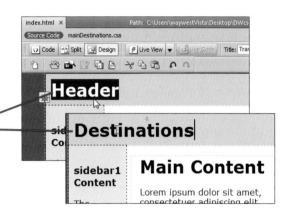

2 As you enter your text in the main column, press [Enter] (Windows) or [Return] (Mac) to start a new paragraph, just as you would with a word processing program. Type in the rest of your text, setting off each line as a separate paragraph. In our example, we've entered a description of the Roman Holiday travel package.

add text (cont.)

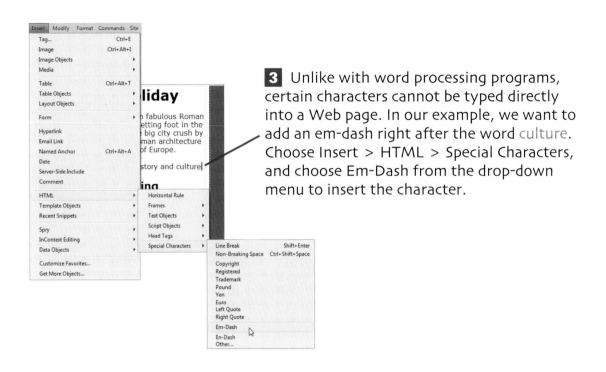

3 Unlike with word processing programs, certain characters cannot be typed directly into a Web page. In our example, we want to add an em-dash right after the word culture. Choose Insert > HTML > Special Characters, and choose Em-Dash from the drop-down menu to insert the character.

Roman Holiday

You can have your own fabulous Roman holididay without ever setting foot in the Eternal City. Avoid the big city crush by exploring the great Roman architecture found across the rest of Europe.

You'll find plenty of history and culture—from Romania's forests to the plains of Spain and the valleys of France.

H2 level heading

4 Once the em-dash is inserted, we can add the rest of the text.

5 Save your changes (Ctrl S in Windows, ⌘ S on the Mac).

insert image placeholder

In a perfect world, all your images would be ready to put into your Web pages right when you're building them. In reality, someone else may be creating the image even though you need to get started building pages. That's why I explain inserting an image placeholder right in the middle of this text-building chapter. You can add the image later (as explained in Chapter 3), but this trick lets you keep working.

1 If you closed your home page previously, reopen it. Click in the header just before its title (Destinations, in our example) and then click the Split view button.

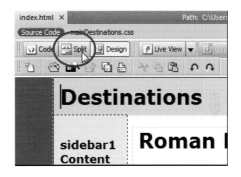

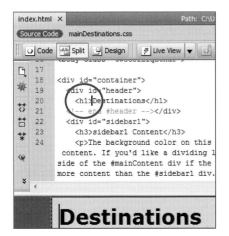

2 We want to insert our company logo here but, as the Split view shows, there's a slight problem. The cursor is sitting after the opening < h1 > header tag. Fix the problem by repositioning your cursor just before the < h1 > tag.

insert placeholder (cont.)

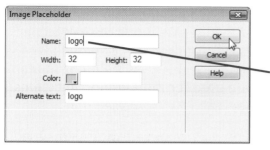

3 From the Menu bar, choose Insert > Image Objects > Image Placeholder. Type in a memory-jogging name for the image-to-come (logo, in our example). If you know the image's exact width and height in pixels, type it in. Otherwise, enter an approximate size for the expected image. Finally, enter Alternate text that briefly describes the image or its function. Click OK to close the dialog box and press F5 to refresh your view.

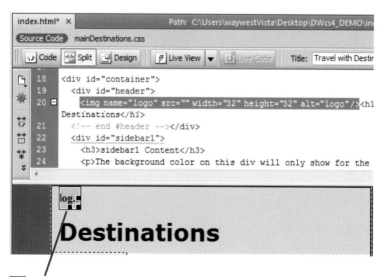

4 Dreamweaver inserts a box into the Web page based on your chosen width and height, helping you gauge how the page will look—and, most importantly, reminding you that you're still missing an image. Close the Split view by clicking the Design button, and save your changes (Ctrl S in Windows, ⌘ S on the Mac).

create headings

Just like newspaper and magazine headlines, headings on a Web page are larger and more noticeable than regular text. They range from size 1 (the largest) to size 6 (the smallest). Whether you're building your own page or using our example page, the basics of creating and changing headings remain the same. Just like a newspaper, larger sizes generally are used for more important items and smaller sizes for less important items. (See extra bits on page 24.)

1 If you closed your home page previously, reopen it. Make sure that you're working in Design view and that the Properties panel is visible (Ctrl F3 in Windows, ⌘ F3 on the Mac).

2 Double-click the first heading in the example page's main column (Roman Holiday) to select it. The Properties panel lists its Format as Heading 1. Another clue about the heading's format can be found in the bottom status bar, where the last tag listed is < h1 >.

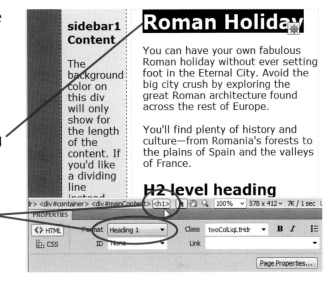

3 Click anywhere in the same column's second heading (H2 level heading), and then click the < h2 > tag in the status bar to select the entire head. As you'd expect, the Properties panel lists its format as Heading 2.

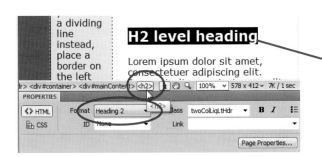

create headings (cont.)

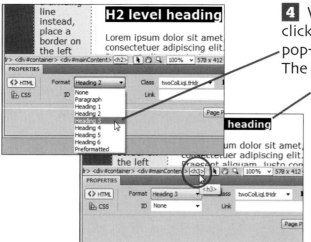

4 With the heading still selected, click the Properties panel's Format pop-up menu and select Heading 3. The heading shrinks to reflect the new, smaller size, and the tag in the status bar changes to < h3 >.

5 Now replace the heading's text by typing in your own (Getting Around in our example). We'll also replace the text below the heading with related text.

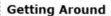

Getting Around

If you want to tool around on a little Vespa, as Audrey Hepburn did in Rome, we're ready for you. Or if a compact camper is more your style, Gregory Peck just might want to go along

6 While we're at it, let's change the sidebar header to a Heading 4, which will look better with the main column heads. In our example, we've also renamed it Services. Don't mess with any of the other settings, such as Font or Style, which we'll fix in a later chapter using Cascading Style Sheets. Save your changes by choosing File > Save ([Ctrl][S] in Windows, [⌘][S] on the Mac).

create lists

Organizing information into lists, whether numbered or simply marked with bullets, makes it easy to group lots of items in a way that anyone can instantly recognize. Ordered lists are great when you need to highlight a specific sequence of steps or materials. We'll quickly show you how to do ordered and unordered lists. We'll cover the rest of the list styling, however, in Chapter 6.

1 Return to your home page and, if it's not already visible, open the Properties panel (Window > Properties) and select everything below the heading in the sidebar.

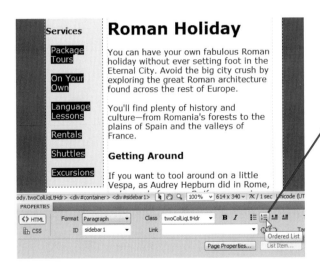

2 Type in your sidebar items, separating each with a paragraph return. Our example lists services available from the travel agency. Select all the items, and click the Ordered List button in the Properties panel. The selected lines will be numbered in sequence from 1 to 6 below the Services heading.

create lists (cont.)

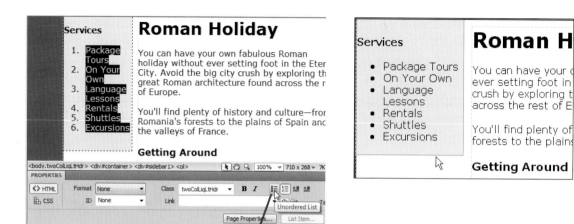

3 Reselect the items, and click the Unordered List button in the Properties panel. The items now have small bullets instead, which in our example more clearly indicates that these are examples of available services. Save your changes (⌈Ctrl⌉⌈S⌉ in Windows, ⌘⌈S⌉ on the Mac).

add a footer

Tucked at the bottom of pages, footers offer a perfect place for displaying essential information that doesn't need to immediately grab a reader's attention. Copyright and contact information are good examples. Thanks to our example's CSS-based layout, the home page already contains a footer. For now, we'll keep it simple, though later we'll use CSS to add some fancier formatting and navigation links.

1 Scroll to the bottom of the example page and select the layout's placeholder text.

2 Replace it by typing in your own text. In our example, that includes the formal name of the business, plus copyright information. (You'll find the © by choosing Insert > HTML > Special Characters.)

3 When you're done, click the CSS button in the Properties panel, and then click the Align Center button to put the text across the bottom-middle of the page. Be sure to save your changes (⌃S in Windows, ⌘S on the Mac).

extra bits

create a home page p. 12

- While this layout is used throughout the book, feel free to choose another of the many pre-designed layouts found under the Blank Page-HTML choice. The principles explained in each chapter can be applied to any of these layouts. Using style sheet–based layouts is the most flexible way to build your site pages. Frames-based layouts are hard to update, difficult to bookmark, and rightly fading in popularity. Layer-based layouts should be avoided as well.

- Naming your CSS file after its related Web site helps reduce confusion if you create more sites (and related CSS files) later on. By the way, don't name the style sheet based on your site's current layout because you'll inevitably tweak the configuration and won't want to keep updating the name.

- The page's file name and title serve different purposes. The file name is used behind the scenes to help you and Dream-weaver keep track of how your files are organized. For example, home pages should always be named index, which helps Web servers know that this page is

the "front door" to your site. The page title is what the viewer's Web browser displays when your page is onscreen.

add text p. 15

- Macintosh computers display Web page text at about three-fourths the size that it appears on a Windows machine, so if you are building your Web site on a Windows PC, avoid the two smallest text sizes.

- To see all 99 special characters that are available, choose Insert > HTML > Special Characters > Other.

- To reach the special characters more easily, you can switch the Insert bar tab from Common to Text, then click the far-right button and choose from the drop-down menu.

create headings p. 19

- To keep your pages uncluttered, limit yourself to no more than two or three heading sizes on the same page.

3. add images

While text and headlines lend structure and meaning to Web pages, it's images that give your pages real impact.

Dreamweaver can handle basic image editing; for more demanding tasks use a dedicated graphics program. Two obvious options are Adobe's own Photoshop and Fireworks programs, available individually or included in some versions of the Dreamweaver CS4 suite. With Photoshop, you can drag images directly into Dreamweaver. For other options, take a look in the graphics section of www.versiontracker.com, where you can compare prices, features, and user comments.

image tools

You'll use the Properties panel as your main tool for most image work. (See extra bits on page 44.) While you can use the Edit buttons to optimize or resample an image, that work is best done with a dedicated graphics program (such as Fireworks or Photoshop) before you begin laying out your Web pages.

Displayed near the image thumbnail is the file size (20K in our example) and its W (width) and H (height) in pixels.

Src tells you where the image is stored, while Link tells you what file (if any) the image is linked to if clicked.

Alt lets you create a label to be read aloud by browsers created for visually handicapped visitors. Also use Alt to describe an image for visitors who have turned off image downloading for speedier surfing.

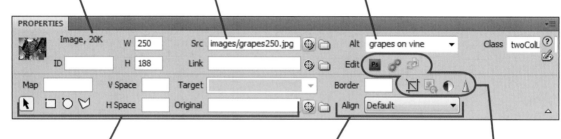

The items from Map to Target are used to create image maps, as explained on page 67.

Avoid using the Properties panel's Border or Align setting; these settings are better handled using the CSS panel group, as explained on page 77.

The first button in the top row indicates your primary image program (set to Photoshop in our example using Preferences > File Types/Editors). Within Dreamweaver, you'll mostly use the next row's Crop, Resample, Contrast/Brightness, and Sharpen buttons.

add image

After sizing and then optimizing images in an external graphics program, you're ready to add the Web-ready versions to your Web pages.

1 Open the page in which you want to add an image. (In our example, we're once again using index.html, the home page created in the previous chapter, and we're working in Dreamweaver's Classic workspace.)

2 Make sure the Insert toolbar's Common tab is selected, and position your cursor at the beginning of the main text.

3 Choose Image from the Image button's drop-down menu.

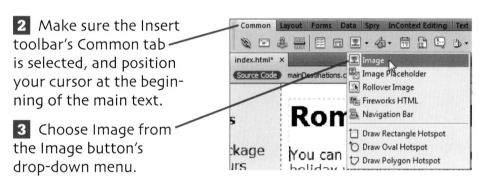

4 When the Select Image Source dialog appears, navigate to the image you want to use, and click OK/Choose. (In our example, we're using janustemple200.jpg.)

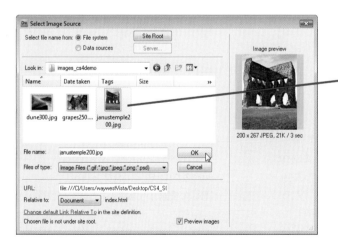

add image (cont.)

5 If the image isn't already a part of your Web site, Dreamweaver asks if you want to save it in the site's root folder. Choose Yes, create a new folder in the site named images, and save the image there. Type a brief description of the image in the Alternate text box when the dialog appears and click OK. (See the "add image" extra bits on page 44.)

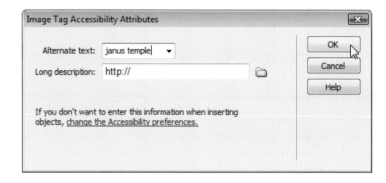

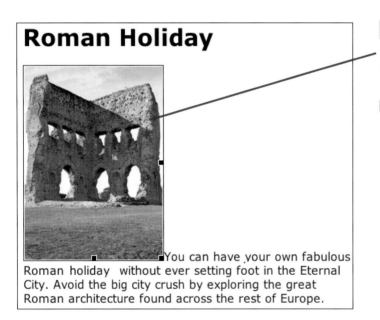

Roman Holiday

You can have your own fabulous Roman holiday without ever setting foot in the Eternal City. Avoid the big city crush by exploring the great Roman architecture found across the rest of Europe.

6 When the image appears on the page, save your work (Ctrl S in Windows, ⌘ S on the Mac).

add flash video

It's easy to add an Adobe Flash video to a Dreamweaver Web page. We'll look at how to handle two different file types. A .swf file runs automatically and is commonly used for a Web site's introduction. A .flv file contains a control panel that users click to start the video.

1 Make sure the Insert toolbar's Common tab is selected. Click in the page where you want to insert either type of Flash file. (In our example, we're working in Dreamweaver's Classic workspace and using movieExamples.html, a mostly blank duplicate of index.html.)

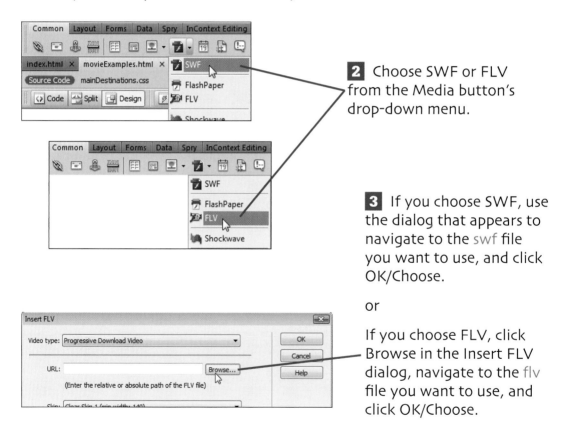

2 Choose SWF or FLV from the Media button's drop-down menu.

3 If you choose SWF, use the dialog that appears to navigate to the swf file you want to use, and click OK/Choose.

or

If you choose FLV, click Browse in the Insert FLV dialog, navigate to the flv file you want to use, and click OK/Choose.

add images

add flash video (cont.)

4 If the image isn't already a part of your Web site, Dreamweaver asks if you want to save it in the site's root folder. Choose Yes, navigate to the site's images folder you created on page 28, and save the image there. When asked, type a brief description of the image in the Title text box and click OK. (See the first "add flash video" extra bit on page 44.)

If you are using a swf file, Dreamweaver immediately inserts a placeholder on the page. Skip to step 6.

or

If you are using a flv file, the Insert FLV dialog reappears, so go to step 5.

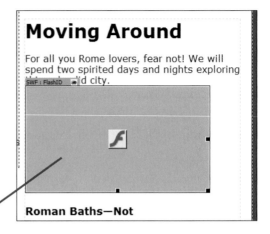

5 If you are using a flv file, leave the Video type set to Progressive Download Video and use the pop-up menu to choose a Skin style for the control buttons that will appear with the video. (In our example, we're using Clear Skin 1, the least obtrusive choice.) Click the Detect Size button once to see the video's natural width and height. If that size is too wide for your Web page, type in a smaller width and height. Click OK when you're done.

Dreamweaver inserts a placeholder for the flv file on the page.

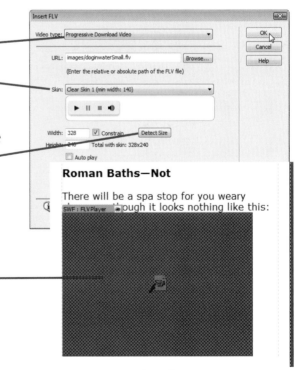

add images

6 Click the Live View button in the Document toolbar to preview either Flash video. The swf file automatically runs as an embedded video. The flv file appears with the start-stop controls you chose in step 5. To stop the video, click the Live View button a second time.

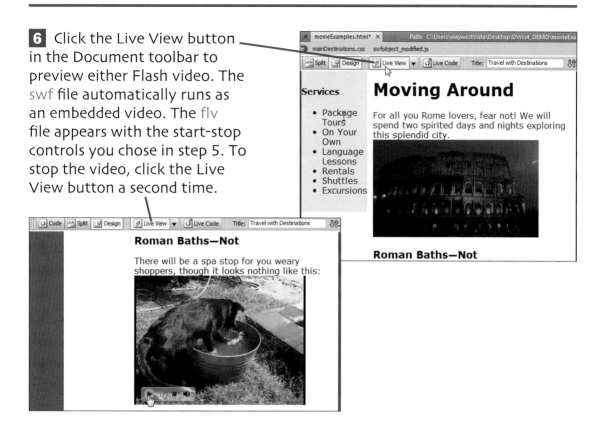

Roman Baths—Not

7 Save your work (Ctrl S in Windows, ⌘ S on the Mac). Click OK when a note explains that two scripts related to the swf video must also be uploaded when you eventually publish your Web site. The two files are added to your local site in a new Scripts folder. (See the second "add flash video" extra bit on page 44.) If you inserted a flv video, two files related to the skin controls are added.

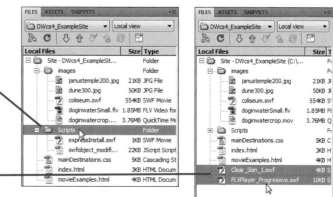

add images

add quicktime video

The process for adding a QuickTime video, or any video or audio file, is similar to the previous steps for Flash: Choose Plugin from the Media button's drop-down menu, navigate to the image you want to use, and select it.

1 Make sure the Insert toolbar's Common tab is selected and that you've opened the page where you want to insert a Quick-Time video. (In our example, we're using movieExamples.html, the same page we used to insert Flash videos.)

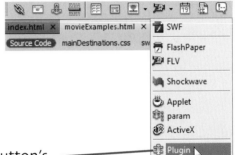

2 Choose Plugin from the Media button's drop-down menu, then use the dialog to navigate to the QuickTime file you want to use, and click OK/Choose.

or

If the QuickTime file is already in your site folder, you can click and drag it from the Files tab directly onto the page.

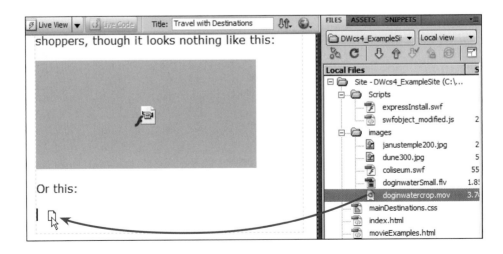

3 Dreamweaver adds a placeholder to the page, and the Properties panel Src window automatically displays the file's name and location.

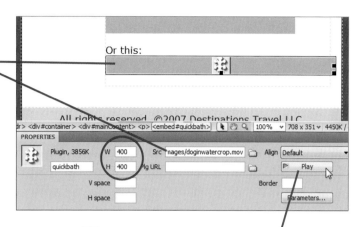

4 Use the width and height text windows to size the image to fit your page, then click Play.

5 The video plays right on your page in Dreamweaver. Click Stop in the Properties panel when you're ready and save your work (Ctrl S in Windows, ⌘ S on the Mac).

add images 33

crop image

You don't need a separate graphics program for cropping images—just don't use your original image unless you create a backup duplicate. Cropping permanently alters your image, so if you make a mistake, immediately choose Undo Crop in the Edit menu. (See the first "crop image" extra bit on page 44.)

1 In the Files tab, select the still image you previously used on page 27 (janustemple200.jpg in our example). Make a copy of it ([Ctrl][D] in Windows, [⌘][D] on the Mac). Dreamweaver automatically adds a duplicate to the tab's list and names it Copy of the file name.

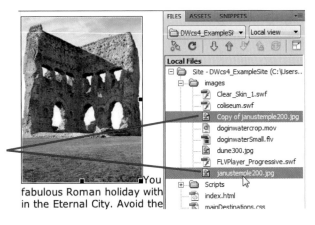

You fabulous Roman holiday with in the Eternal City. Avoid the

2 Reselect the original image in the Web page and click the Crop button in the Properties panel. An alert dialog immediately appears warning that crops are permanent. Click OK since you already made a duplicate of the image.

3 A selection area, marked by a line and darker surrounding area, appears in the middle of the image. Click and drag any of the black handles along the selection's edge to set your crop lines or click-and-drag in the middle to reposition the entire crop.

You can have your ow fabulous Roman holiday without ever setting foot in the Eternal City. Avoid the big city cru by exploring the great Roman architecture fou across the rest of Europe.

Double-click inside the selection and the image is trimmed.

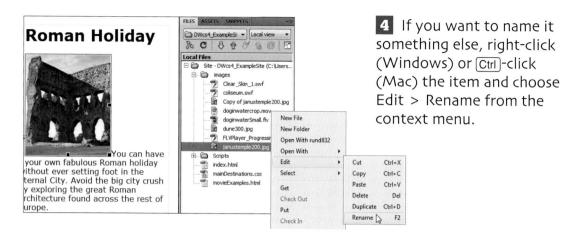

4 If you want to name it something else, right-click (Windows) or Ctrl-click (Mac) the item and choose Edit > Rename from the context menu.

5 Once the name is highlighted, type in a new name and press Enter (Windows) or Return (Mac). (In our example, we use janustemple180.jpg to reflect its new cropped width of 180 pixels.) Dreamweaver needs to update the links to the page to reflect the new name, so click Update. (See the second "crop image" extra bit on page 44.)

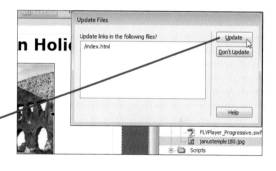

6 The Properties panel's Src box now reflects the new name, janustemple180.jpg. Save your work (Ctrl S in Windows, ⌘ S on the Mac).

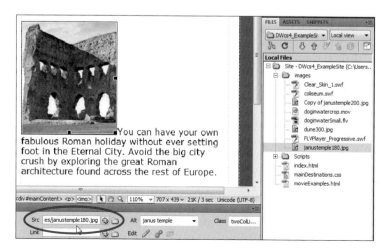

You can have your own fabulous Roman holiday without ever setting foot in the Eternal City. Avoid the big city crush by exploring the great Roman architecture found across the rest of Europe.

adjust brightness

A single button in the Properties panel lets you adjust an image's brightness or contrast. Sometimes minor adjustments of either can really help a so-so image. Assuming you are using the same image from the previous task, you do not need to make another duplicate of the image.

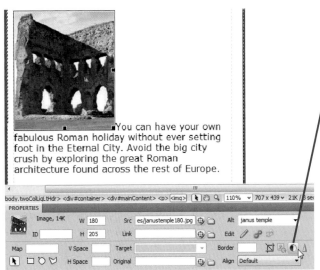

You can have your own fabulous Roman holiday without ever setting foot in the Eternal City. Avoid the big city crush by exploring the great Roman architecture found across the rest of Europe.

1 On your page, click to select the image that you want to adjust (janustemple180.jpg in our example). Click the Contrast/Brightness button in the Properties panel. (Click OK to close the alert dialog since you are already working with a duplicate image.)

2 To change the brightness or contrast drag the sliders or enter new values in the adjacent text windows. (Increase the effects by sliding to the right or entering a larger number.) (See the "adjust brightness" extra bit on page 44.) Click OK to apply your adjustments. Save your work (Ctrl S in Windows, ⌘ S on the Mac).

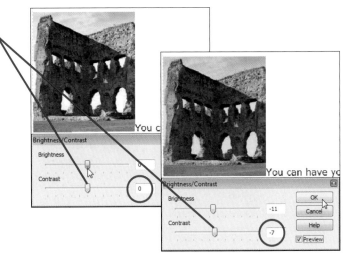

create thumbnail image

If you have an image without lots of details, you can use it to create a tiny thumbnail to add some graphic variety to a page. Detail lost from reducing and resampling cannot be recovered, so use a duplicate of your original image. (See extra bits on page 44.)

1 Click in the page where you want to use the duplicate of your original image (Copy of dune300.jpg in our example in a blank duplicate we created of the index page named dunepage.html). Choose Image from the Image button's drop-down menu to insert the image (or drag the image directly to the page from its listing in the Files tab).

2 Click to select the image, then press Shift as you drag one of the image's corner handles. This reduces the image while maintaining its proportions.

Watch the pixel dimensions change in the W and H text windows in the Properties panel to gauge how much to reduce the image. (In our example, we want reduce the image to a width of 100 pixels.)

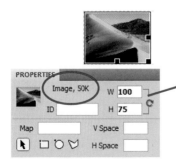

3 Release the cursor and the image appears with the new dimensions in bold—even though the actual size of the file remains the same. The circling arrow connecting the two numbers is meant to remind you of what comes next.

create thumbnail (cont.)

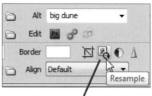

4 Click the Properties panel's Resample button. Click OK when an alert dialog appears warning that the change is permanent since you are using a duplicate image. Dreamweaver then reduces the actual file size, indicated afterward by a smaller K size in the Properties panel.

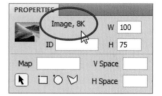

5 Greatly reduced images often lose some crispness, so click the Properties panel's Sharpen button. Click OK when a alert dialog appears warning that the change is permanent since you are using a duplicate image.

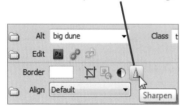

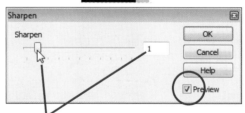

6 Be sure Preview is checked, then use the slider or text window in the Sharpen dialog to adjust the amount. (Drag the slider to the right or enter a higher number in the text window to increase the sharpening.) Click OK when you're satisfied. Save the page before continuing.

add images

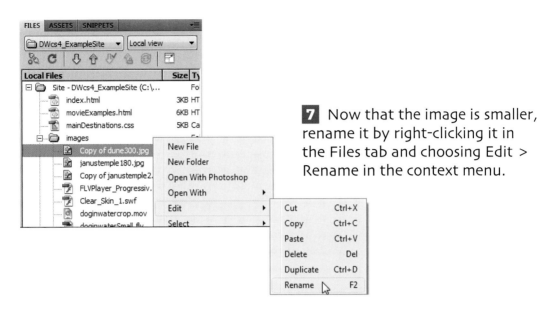

7 Now that the image is smaller, rename it by right-clicking it in the Files tab and choosing Edit > Rename in the context menu.

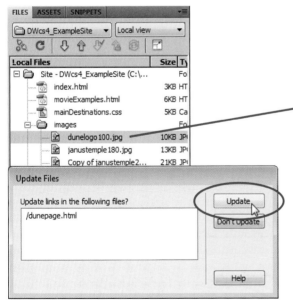

8 Type in a new name while preserving the .jpg suffix. (Our example uses dunelogo100.jpg to reflect the image's new width.) Press [Enter] (Windows) or [Return] (Mac) to apply the change. Click Update when Dreamweaver asks to update links to the renamed image.

add images

replace placeholder

We'll use this process to replace the image placeholder created on page 17 in Chapter 2. It's similar to inserting an image except that the placeholder's Alt text is preserved.

1 Click to select the image placeholder you inserted in Chapter 2 (logo in our example).

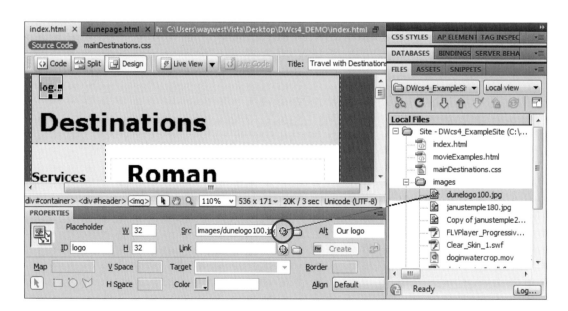

2 In the Properties panel, click the compass-like Point to File button. Drag the line that appears to the image that will replace the placeholder (dunelogo100.jpg in our example), and release the cursor.

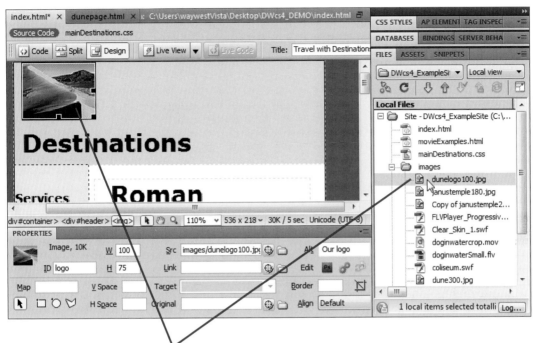

3 The new image instantly replaces the placeholder. Save your work ([Ctrl][S] in Windows, [⌘][S] on the Mac).

flow text around images

Wrapping blocks of text around your images creates a tighter, more professional page layout. In previous versions of Dreamweaver, the Properties panel was the tool used most often to wrap text around images. However, using the CSS Styles tab instead gives you more control, and makes it easier to update those styles as needed. Don't worry, we're simply going to apply some existing CSS rules to get our feet wet. The big CSS plunge comes in Chapter 6.

1 Click to select an image already inserted into a page's text. (In our example, it's janustemple180.jpg, which is linked to an existing style sheet, mainDestinations.css.) Make sure the CSS Styles panel is visible (Window > CSS Styles) and set to All.

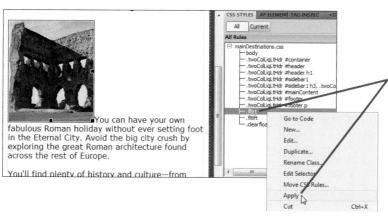

2 Near the bottom of the list of CSS rules, right-click the rule called .fltrt and choose Apply from the context menu.

add images

3 The selected image floats to the right side of the page with a bit of space separating it from the words now on the left. That's because the .fltrt rule has two properties: a right float and a left margin of 8px (pixels).

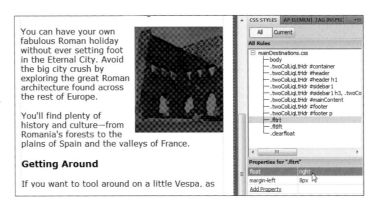

4 Insert another image farther down the page (grapes250.jpg from the images folder in our example). In the CSS Styles list, right-click the rule called .fltlft and select Apply from the context menu.

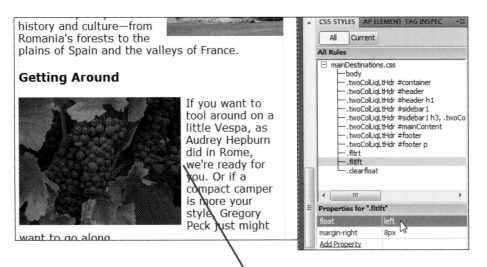

The image floats to the left with the same 8-pixel margin down the right side, exactly the properties listed for the .fltlft rule. Save your work ((Ctrl)(S) in Windows, (⌘)(S) on the Mac).

extra bits

image tools p. 26

- Ignore the blank ID text window to the right of the Properties panel's thumbnail image, which is for scripts.

add image p. 27

- The root folder contains all your Web site's files. (In our example, it's DWcs4_ExampleSite.) An images subfolder within the root folder makes it easier to find your photos or graphics.
- Always add Alt text for your images. Special audio Web browsers also use Alt text for visually impaired visitors. If the image is something like a horizontal rule, choose < empty > from the drop-down menu.

add flash video p. 29

- In step 4, if the swf or flv file already is in your site folder, you can click and drag it from the Files tab directly onto the page.
- In step 7, when Dreamweaver adds the swf scripts, it also displays the related JavaScript file in the Related Files toolbar just below the tab for your video page.

crop image p. 34

- In our example, we crop an image already inserted into a page. You also can open an image directly from the Files panel, make your crops, and then insert it into a page. Choose the workflow that feels most natural, then stick with it for consistent results.
- It's easy to wind up with several different sizes of the same image for different sections of your layout. By including the image's pixel width at the end of its name, such as janustemple180.jpg, it's easy to remember which is which.

adjust brightness p. 36

- The sliders can be hard to control, so type numbers in the text windows for fine adjustments.

create thumbnail image p. 37

- You could use resampling to enlarge an image, but don't. The quality will suffer noticeably. Instead, use your regular image-editing program with the (presumably) larger original.
- When you click the Resample button, a dialog warns you that the change is permanent. Since we're using a duplicate, click OK.

4. add tables

While it once was common to use tables to create layouts, Cascading Style Sheets thankfully now offer a more powerful and flexible approach. For that reason, this chapter focuses on columnar tables.

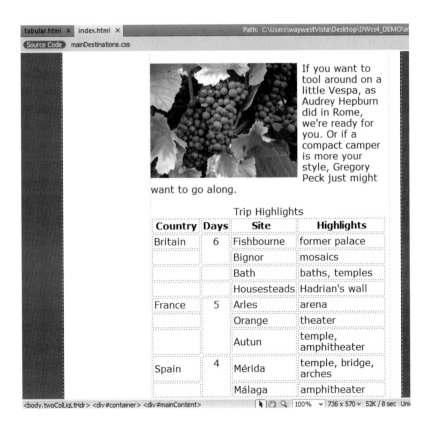

add a table

Tables provide a great way to corral information into easy-to-scan rows and columns.

1 Open the page in which you want to add a table. (In our example, we're once again using index.html, the home page used in the previous chapter.) Make sure that the Properties panel is visible, and that the Insert toolbar's Common tab is selected.

2 Press [Enter] (Windows) or [Return] (Mac) to start a fresh paragraph where you want the table to appear. Click the Table button in the Common tab.

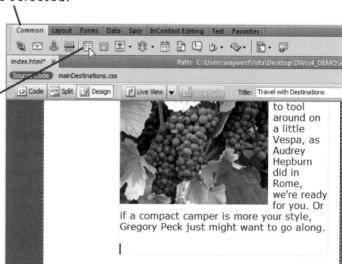

3 When the Table dialog appears, use the text boxes to set the Table width and whether you want to include a Header, which creates boldfaced labels for the darkened cells. (In our example, we've set Rows to 3, Columns to 3, Table width to 400 pixels, Border thickness to 0 and Cell padding to 3 pixels.) Click OK to insert the new table. (See the first two "add a table" extra bits on page 57.)

Use the Accessibility section to create a caption that's used by audio-based Web browsers. (See the third "add a table" extra bit on page 57.)

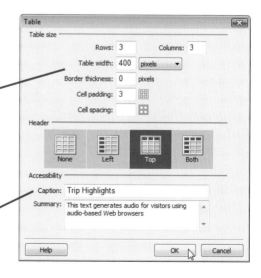

4 When the new table appears, type your labels into the header cells, where they are boldfaced. Type the rest of your table content into each cell. Press Tab to move from cell to cell. Don't bother formatting the text; do it after you read Chapter 6 and it'll be a snap. (See the last "add a table" extra bit on page 57.)

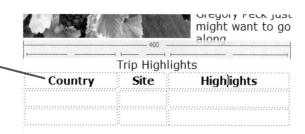

5 If you need more cells as you type, switch the Insert toolbar to the Layout tab.

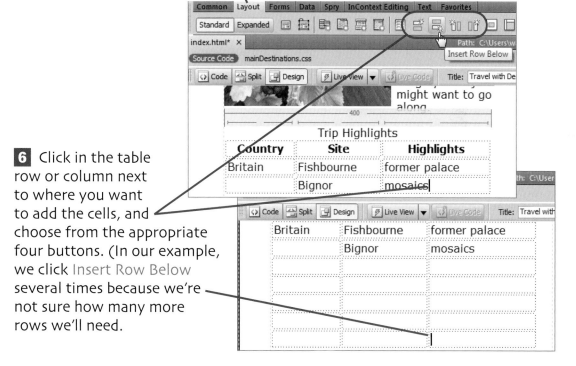

6 Click in the table row or column next to where you want to add the cells, and choose from the appropriate four buttons. (In our example, we click Insert Row Below several times because we're not sure how many more rows we'll need.

7 Finish typing your information into the table. Save your work (Ctrl S in Windows, ⌘S on the Mac).

select, change table parts

Inevitably as you create tables, you'll need to tweak them in various ways, whether it's removing extra rows, adding a column, or moving the whole table. This section covers the changes you'll make most often. For more elaborate formatting options, see Chapter 6.

1 If you've closed it, reopen the page where you added a table in the previous steps and, if necessary, add an extra row using the Insert Row Below button. (Our example table in index.html already has an extra row at the bottom.)

Trip Highlights		
Country	**Site**	**Highlights**
Britain	Fishbourne	former palace
	Bignor	mosaics
France	Arles	arena
	Orange	theater
	Autun	temple, amphitheater
Spain	Mérida	temple, bridge, arches
	Málaga	amphitheater

2 Ordinarily you select a row by moving your cursor to the table's left side whereupon it becomes a big, bold arrow. However, as in our example, a table often sits flush left, making that method difficult. It's easier to use the status bar's tag selector: Click in any cell in that extra row and the cell's tag <td> is highlighted in the status bar. (See the first "select, change table parts" extra bit on page 57.)

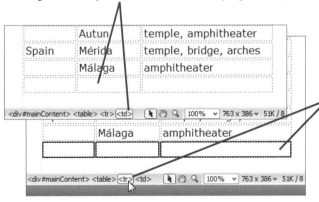

3 Just to the left of the cell's tag is the row's tag <tr>. Click it and the entire row is selected.

4 Press ⟵Backspace (Windows) or Delete (Mac) and the selected row is removed.

add tables

5 To add a new column, move your cursor to the top of a column on either side of where you want it to go. The cursor becomes a bold arrow.

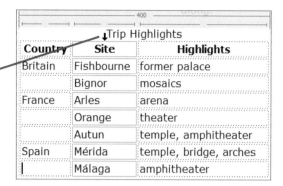

6 In the Layout tab of the Insert toolbar, click one of the two Insert Column buttons to insert a column to the left or right of the selected column. A new blank column is inserted in the table.

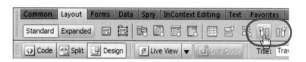

7 Use the status bar's magnify pop-up menu to zoom in a bit on the column so you can add your information.

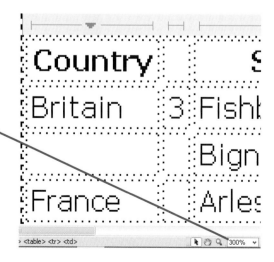

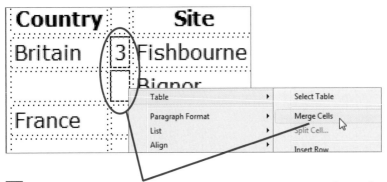

8 If you want to merge several cells into one, drag the cursor across the multiple cells (in our example the 3 and the blank cell below it). Right-click, choose Table > Merge Cells from the context menu, and the cells are merged. (See the second "select, change table parts" extra bit on page 57.)

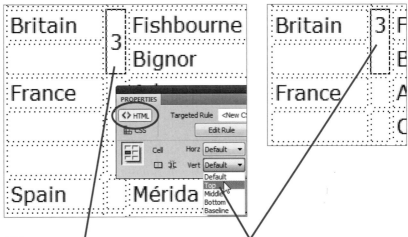

9 After merging cells, you may need to change the content's vertical alignment (in our example the 3 is centered vertically when we want it at the top). With the cells selected, click the Properties panel's HTML button and use the Vert pop-up menu to select a new setting that is applied to the content. Repeat the steps for any other cells you've merged.

10 Remember to type in a header/label for any new columns. It's automatically boldfaced.

11 If you need to adjust the horizontal alignment of a column's text, select the cells, click the Properties panel's Horz pop-up menu, choose a new setting, and it's applied to the content.

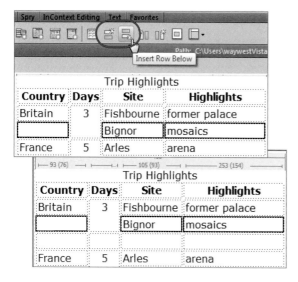

12 To add a row, select the row above or below as explained in steps 2 and 3. In the Layout tab of the Insert toolbar, click one of the two Insert Row buttons, and a new blank row is inserted in the table.

13 Save your work (Ctrl S in Windows, ⌘ S on the Mac), and click the Document toolbar's Globe button to preview the results in various Web browsers.

import tabular data

Nothing beats a table for clearly presenting spreadsheet data or tab-separated text imported from a word-processing document. More importantly, in a world full of tab-delimited data such as Excel spreadsheets, importing such text can save you hours of typing. (See the first "import tabular data" extra bit on page 57.)

1 Open a page into which you want to place tabular data from another program. (In our example, we've duplicated index.html from the previous section and deleted everything in the main content area. After renaming it tabular.html, we've saved it to our example site.)

2 Click in the page where you want the data placed.

Roman Holiday: Details

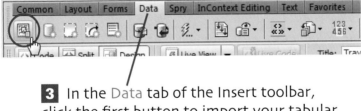

3 In the Data tab of the Insert toolbar, click the first button to import your tabular data. (See the second "import tabular data" extra bit on page 57.)

4 Click Browse to navigate to where you've stored the spreadsheet or word-processing document.

5 For the Delimiter, use Tab (or whatever format you used when saving the document you're now importing). In the Table width section, choose Set to and use the adjacent text windows to specify that width (90 percent in our example) Skip the padding and spacing settings, set the Format top row to [No Formatting] and click OK.

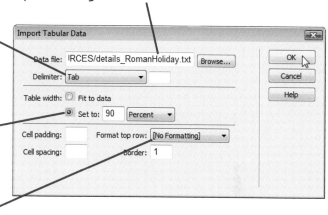

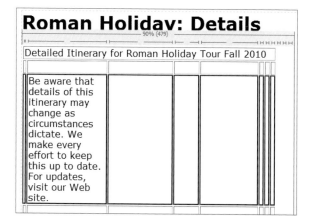

6 The data appears on the Web page arranged in its own table. Inevitably, our example table has a few errors. The same methods covered in the previous section work for the imported table, so clean up as needed.

import tabular data (cont.)

7 In general, resist the urge to apply a lot of formatting to the imported table since that's best done using style sheets, as explained in Chapter 6. However, in our example, after selecting the table's header, we click the Properties panel's HTML button and then apply the Heading 4 format. In Chapter 6, we'll show how to use CSS to further define headings in a specific context, such as tables.

8 Save your work page (Ctrl S in Windows, ⌘ S on the Mac), and click the Document toolbar's Globe button to preview the results in various Web browsers.

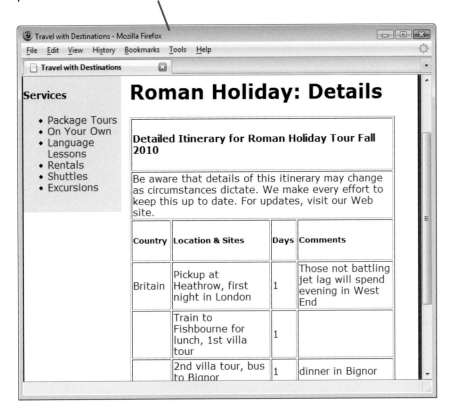

sort tables

Dreamweaver can automatically sort tabular data by column—a neat trick that lets you tinker with how the data is organized long after you've imported it into your table. There's just one catch: tables cannot be sorted if they include any cells spanning multiple columns, such as the merged cells in our current example. With a quick cut and paste, however, it's easy to work around this restriction as long as the merged cells are not scattered through the table.

1 Select the part of your table without any merged cells. (In our example, it's everything below the "Be aware" note.) Cut it from the page (Ctrl X in Windows, ⌘ X on the Mac).

Roman Holiday: Details

Detailed Itinerary for Roman Holiday Tour Fall 2010			
Be aware that details of this itinerary may change as circumstances dictate. We make every effort to keep this up to date. For updates, visit our Web site.			

Roman Holiday: Details

Detailed Itinerary for Roman Holiday Tour Fall 2010			
Country	Location & Sites	Days	Comments
Britain	Pickup at Heathrow, first night in London	1	Those not battling jet lag will spend evening in West End
	Train to Fishbourne for lunch, 1st villa tour	1	
	2nd villa tour, bus to Bignor	1	dinner in Bignor
	am lecture on Roman mosaics		
	Bath	2	

2 Once the section is cut, click just below the remaining part of the table and repaste the deleted portion (Ctrl V in Windows, ⌘ V on the Mac).

The material reappears as a separate table, which you can now sort.

Use the status bar's tag selector to click the < table > tag, then choose Commands > Sort Table to open the Sort Table dialog.

Detailed Itinerary for Roman Holiday Tour Fall 2010			
Be aware that details of this itinerary may change as circumstances dictate. We make every effort to keep this up to date. For updates, visit our Web site.			
Country	Location & Sites	Days	Comments
Britain	Pickup at Heathrow, first night in London	1	Those not battling jet lag will spend evening in West End
	Train to Fishbourne for lunch, 1st villa tour	1	
	2nd villa tour, bus to Bignor	1	dinner in Bignor
	am lecture on Roman mosaics		
	Bath	2	
	Train to Housesteads	1	Hadrian's wall, night train to Heathrow

sort tables (cont.)

3 Use the Sort by drop-down menu to choose which column controls the sort, then use the Order drop-down menu to set whether the sort is done Alphabetically (or Numerically) and whether it's in Ascending (or Descending) order. In our example, we sort by Column 3 (Days). We also set Then by to sort using Column 1 (Country). Click Apply to preview the sort. (See the "sort tables" extra bit on the next page.)

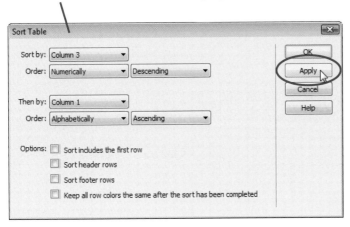

4 Dreamweaver sorts the table based on your choices. Adjust the Sort Table choices if necessary and click Apply once again. When you're satisfied, click OK to close the dialog.

Country	Location & Sites	Days	Comments
Total Days		6	
	Bath	2	
	2nd villa tour, bus to Bignor	1	dinner in Bignor
	Train to Fishbourne for lunch, 1st villa tour	1	
	Train to Housesteads	1	Hadrian's wall, night train to Heathrow

extra bits

add a table p. 46

- The first time you use the Table dialog it's set for three rows and columns. After that it displays the settings used for the last table you created.

- Setting the border thickness at 1 or 2 pixels (or 0 as in our example) creates a cleaner, more open look.

- Use the Table dialog's Accessibility section to create an explanatory Caption that is read aloud by special audio Web browsers for visually impaired visitors. If needed, add details in the Summary field.

- Table cells can hold images, as well as text: The steps for inserting images into a cell are the same as those in Chapter 3.

select, change table parts p. 48

- If you're having trouble selecting a table, click the < table > tag down in the status bar.

- To split a single cell into two cells, right-click inside it, and in the context menu choose Table > Split Cell.

import tabular data p. 52

- Before importing, use your spreadsheet or word-processing program to save the data in comma- or tab-delimited form.

- Instead of using the Import Tabular Data button in the Data tab, you also can choose Insert > Table Objects > Import Tabular Data.

sort tables p. 55

- By default, the Options in the Sort Table dialog are not checked, since you seldom want the header or footer included in the sort.

5. create links

The Web's magic comes largely from the hyperlink, which lets Web users jump from page to image to email to almost anywhere on the Internet. Links fall into two categories: internal links, which connect different items within your own Web site, and external links, which connect to items out on the larger Web. Before we begin linking some of the pages created in previous chapters, switch the Insert toolbar/panel to the Common tab, which includes link-related buttons.

Add link   Add anchor link

Add email link

link text internally

Dreamweaver makes creating links between pages on your Web site a point-and-click affair.

1 Open your home page and select text you want to link to another page on your Web site. (In our example, we are linking the word Europe in the Roman Holiday package to a day-by-day itinerary, tabular.html.)

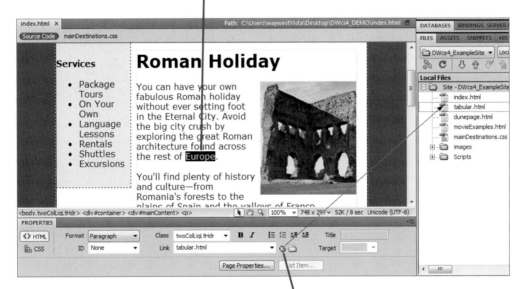

2 Make sure the Files panel and the Properties panel are both visible.

3 Click the compass-like Point to File icon and drag the line that appears to your target file in the Files panel. Release your cursor and the file path to that file appears in the Link text window. (See the "link text internally" extra bit on page 75.)

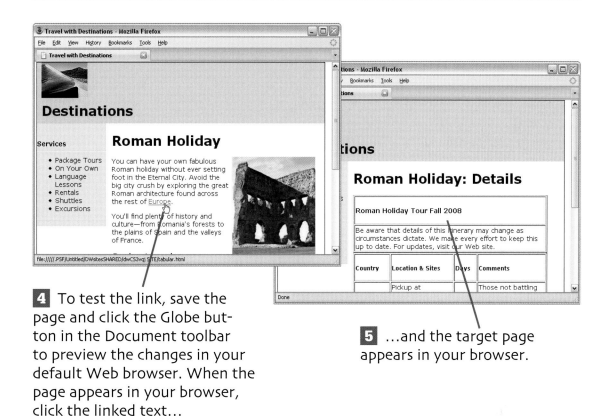

4 To test the link, save the page and click the Globe button in the Document toolbar to preview the changes in your default Web browser. When the page appears in your browser, click the linked text...

5 ...and the target page appears in your browser.

link text externally

Links to items that are not part of your own Web site are called external links. While we use text in this example, you can create external links using images as well.

1 Make sure the Properties panel is visible, then select the text you want to link to a page out on the Web.

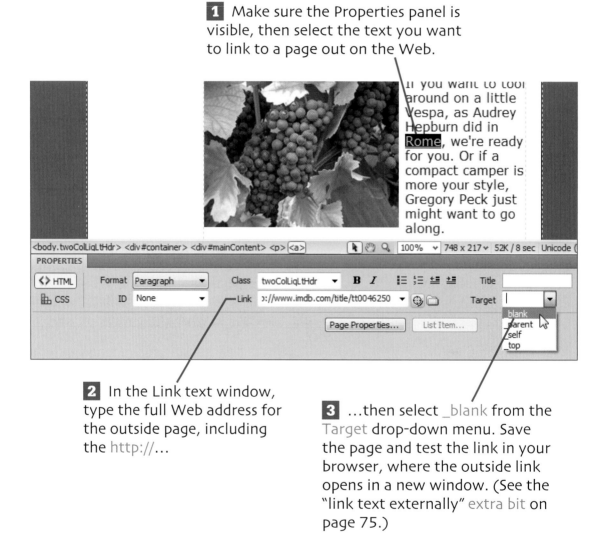

2 In the Link text window, type the full Web address for the outside page, including the http://...

3 ...then select _blank from the Target drop-down menu. Save the page and test the link in your browser, where the outside link opens in a new window. (See the "link text externally" extra bit on page 75.)

add email link

By embedding addresses in your email links, you make it easy for readers to send email to you and others listed on your Web site. Unfortunately, you also make it easier for spammers with Web-crawler programs to pick up that address and flood it with spam. For another approach, see create form on page 106.

1 Select the text on your page that you want to link to email. (In our example, we've selected Rentals from the page's sidebar of available services.)

2 Click the Email Link button under the Common tab of the Insert toolbar/panel.

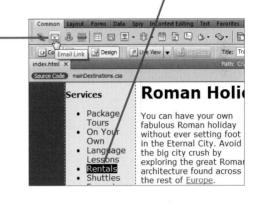

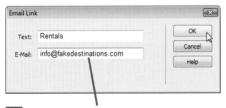

3 The selected text appears in the top field in the Email Link dialog. Type the email address into the bottom field and click OK.

4 The text selected on your page becomes a link. Test it by saving the page, opening it in your Web browser, and clicking the link. Your default email program automatically creates a new message addressed to the email address on the Web page.

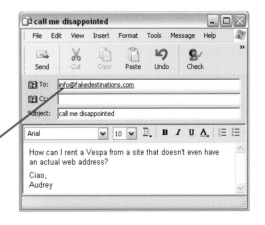

add anchor link

Anchor links enable Web visitors to jump to a specific spot within a long Web page, sparing readers from scrolling through it. You must first create an anchor to mark the particular spot in the target document. Then you create a link to that spot.

1 Open a Web page and click on the particular spot—not selecting the text itself—where you want to add an anchor link. (In our example, we're marking the start of the France section of tabular.html.) (See the first "add anchor link" extra bit on page 75.)

2 Click the Named Anchor button in the Common tab of the Insert toolbar/panel.

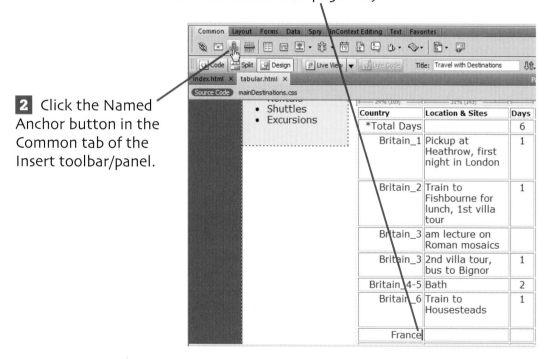

3 Type a distinctive name in the Named Anchor dialog and click OK.

4 An anchor icon is added next to the spot you chose in step 1. Save the page, which also saves the anchor name. (See the second "add anchor link" extra bit on page 75.)

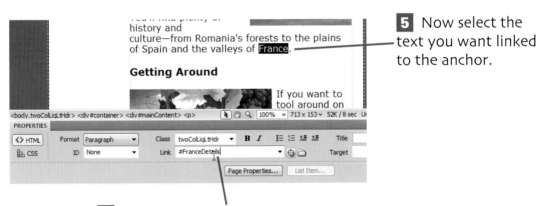

5 Now select the text you want linked to the anchor.

6 In the Properties panel's Link text window, type # and (with no space between) the exact anchor name you created in step 3 (#FranceDetails in our example). Press Enter (Windows) or Return (Mac) to activate the link.

create links

link image

Images are easy to spot on a page and easy to click, so don't limit yourself to creating just text links. Creating internal and external links with images works exactly as it does for text links.

1 With the Files panel and Properties panel both visible, open the page containing the image you want to link to something, and select it.

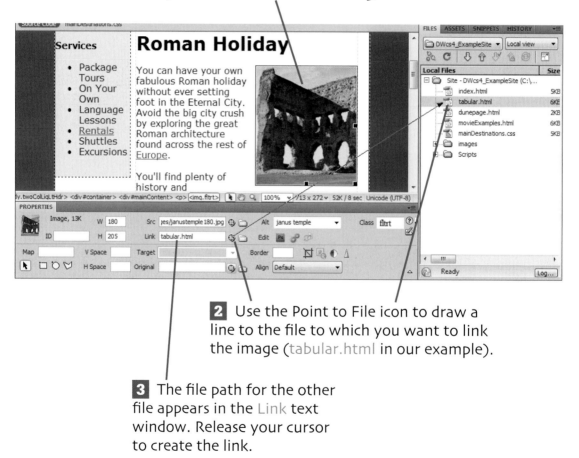

2 Use the Point to File icon to draw a line to the file to which you want to link the image (tabular.html in our example).

3 The file path for the other file appears in the Link text window. Release your cursor to create the link.

create links

create image map

Image maps take the basic idea behind an image link and give it extra power by making it possible to link separate hot spots within the image to multiple files. It saves space on the page and provides an elegant, easy-to-understand interface for your site. (In our example, we're using an already created page named take_your_pick.html.)

1 With the Properties panel visible, select the image for which you want to create an image map. Type a name for the image map in the Map text window (Europe in our example). (See the first "create image map" extra bit on page 75.)

2 Based on the shape of the hot spot you'll be creating, click one of the three shape buttons (the Oval tool in our example).

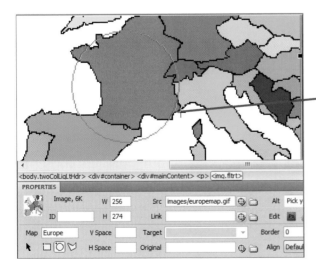

3 Click in your image where you want the hot spot to begin, drag the cursor in a continuous motion, and release. (See the second "create image map" extra bit on page 75.)

create image map (cont.)

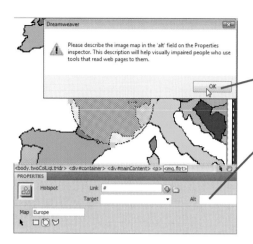

4 The instant you release the cursor, a warning dialog appears. Click OK to close it, and in the Properties panel, name the spot using the Alt text window (we'll enter France in our example).

5 Use the Point to File icon to link the hot spot to a document (tabular.html in our example). (See the third and fourth "create image map" extra bits on page 75.)

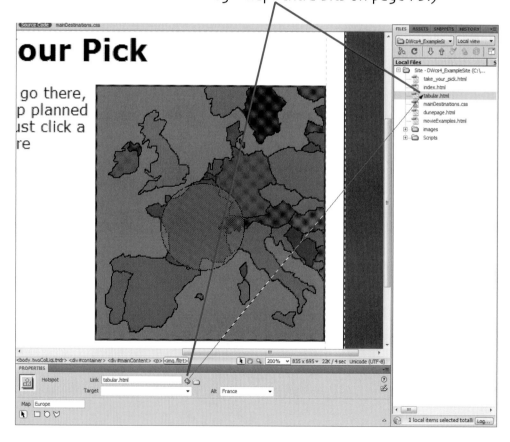

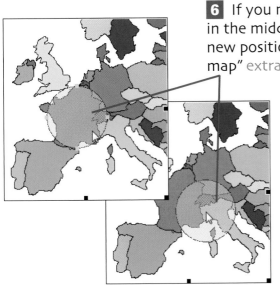

6 If you need to move the hot spot, click in the middle of the spot and drag it to a new position. (See the last "create image map" extra bits on page 75.)

7 Repeat these steps for each hot spot you need to create. Be sure to add an Alt name for each hot spot to help you keep them straight.

8 To test the link, save the page, and launch your default Web browser by clicking the Document toolbar's Globe button to preview the results. Roll the cursor over any of the image's hot spots and the name of the linked file appears in the Status bar.

9 Click the spot and the linked page appears in your browser.

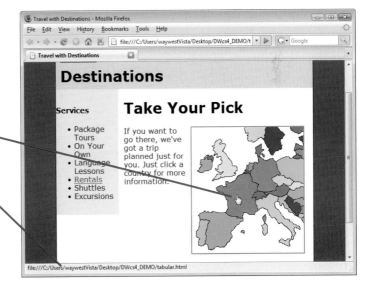

color site links

By default, unvisited Web links are blue and underlined while visited links are purple and underlined. Dreamweaver, however, makes it easy to change the color and style of all your links to match your Web site's overall look. Here we'll set colors for all four link states: unvisited link, visited, hover, and active.

1 Open your home page, make sure your CSS Styles tab is visible, and click the New CSS Rule button.

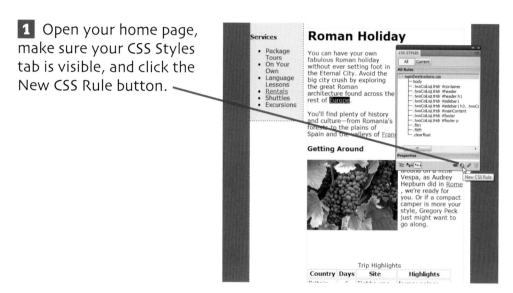

2 In the New CSS Rule dialog, change the Selector Type to Compound and use the Selector Name drop-down menu to choose a:link. (The external style sheet, mainDestinations.css, is automatically chosen.) Click OK to close the dialog.

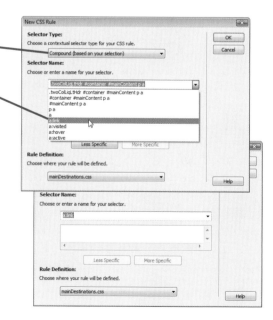

create links

3 When the CSS Rule Definition dialog opens, the Type category is automatically selected. Click the Color box and use the drop-down menu to choose a color for your hyperlinks.

4 Click OK to close the dialog.

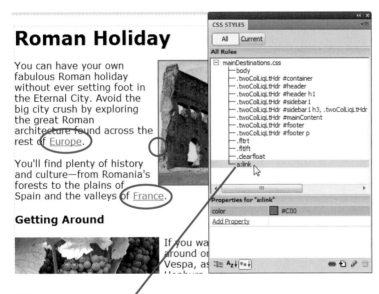

5 The new a:link rule is added to the style sheet list and the page's links assume the new color. But there are two problems: the links are underlined, when we don't want them to be, and the linked image shows a colored border, which we also don't want. We'll fix the underline problem first by double-clicking the a:link rule to reopen the rule definition dialog.

6 By default, the Type category remains selected. Change the Text-decoration checkbox from underline to none.

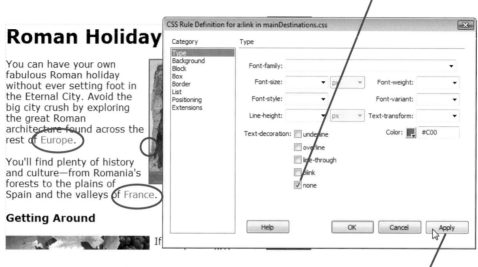

Roman Holiday

You can have your own fabulous Roman holiday without ever setting foot in the Eternal City. Avoid the big city crush by exploring the great Roman architecture found across the rest of Europe.

You'll find plenty of history and culture—from Romania's forests to the plains of Spain and the valleys of France.

Getting Around

7 Position the dialog so that you can see your page, click Apply, and the page links lose the underlines (though the image's colored border remains). Click OK to close the dialog.

8 Let's get rid of the linked image's colored border. When the CSS Styles tab reappears, select the image and click the New CSS Rule button as you did in step 1.

9 In the New CSS Rule dialog, set the Selector Type to Tag and the Selector Name text window automatically displays img (for image). By default, the Rule Definition section lists your main external style sheet (mainDestinations.css in our example).

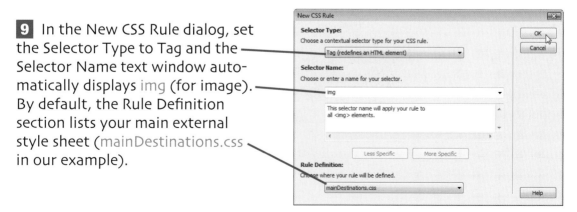

10 Change the category from Type to Border.

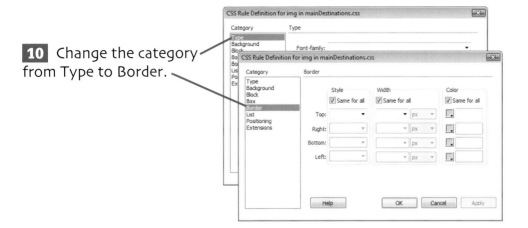

11 In the Style column, set the Top text window to none. In the Width column, type 0 (zero) in the Top window; the pixels measure then appears automatically. Position the dialog so that you can see your page, click Apply, and the image's border disappears.

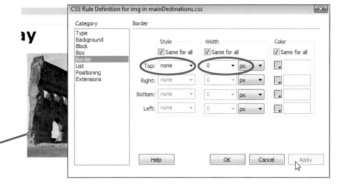

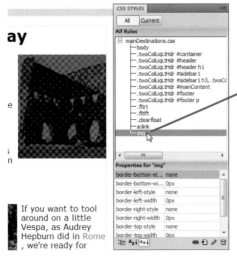

12 Click OK to close the dialog, and the new img rule appears at the bottom of the CSS Styles tab. Choose File > Save All to save the changes to the content and style sheet.

If you want to tool around on a little Vespa, as Audrey Hepburn did in Rome, we're ready for

create links

color site links (cont.)

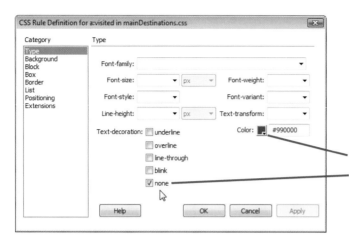

13 With those cleanups out of the way, repeat steps 1–6 to create and define rules for the remaining three link states: a:visited, a:hover, and a:active. Just remember while setting each state's link Color to also set Text-decoration to none at the same time.

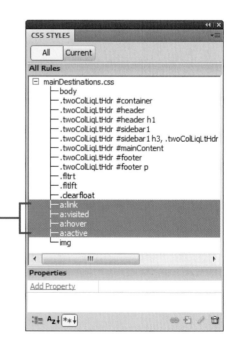

14 Choose File > Save All to save all your content and style changes. When you're done, all four link styles are listed in your main external style sheet (mainDestinations.css in our example). These are applied to any hyperlinks in pages attached to the style sheet, as explained in the next chapter.

create links

extra bits

link text internally p. 60

- If the file to which you're linking is not already part of your Web site, click the Folder icon next to the Link drop-down menu and navigate to it. When Dreamweaver asks to import the file into the site, click Yes.

link text externally p. 62

- Selecting _blank from the Target drop-down menu opens a new window in the visitor's browser— ensuring that your site remains visible as the visitor looks at the external Web page.

add anchor link p. 64

- The anchor doesn't need to be tied to a text selection.

- Dreamweaver inserts an icon next to your anchor-link text just to help you spot it. It will not be visible on your Web site. To turn these icons off or on, choose View > Visual Aids > Invisible Elements.

create image map p. 67

- Image map names should not include any blank spaces or special characters.

- The hot spot need not exactly match the underlying shape. Just cover the portion your visitors will most likely click.

- If you can't arrange your document windows to point directly to an anchor, click the folder button in the Properties panel to reach the file. At the end of the file name selected in the Link text window, type # and the exact name of the anchor (without a space).

- A hot spot can link to an internal or external file.

- To expand or shrink the hot spot, click in its middle, click any one of the square-shaped handles that appear, and drag it outward or inward. It can be tricky activating the handles, so zoom in a bit on the image to better see what's going on.

6. use style sheets

In previous chapters, you saw how Cascading Style Sheets (CSS) save you time in creating and formatting pages. Using those examples, you learned how to change and create style rules. In this chapter, we go a bit deeper, formatting elements based on their use or context.

You'll learn to create a variety of styles to cover virtually all your needs. Tag-based styles, also known as element-based styles, apply to a specific HTML element, such as every h1 or li tag. Compound styles—also know as context-based styles—enable you to apply a style when a certain combination of tags appears in a specific context, such as the page's header or sidebar. Finally, class-based styles are not pegged to a particular tag and, so, can be applied to multiple items anywhere in a page. If you want to learn still more about CSS after reading this chapter, check out Peachpit's Dreamweaver CS4: Visual QuickStart Guide on page xiv.

using the css styles tab

Dreamweaver conveniently puts everything you need for creating and managing style sheets in the CSS Styles tab. Along with the Files tab, it's something you'll always want visible. In contrast, you're unlikely to ever use the AP Elements tab, which is grouped in the same CSS panel. (See the "using the css styles tab" extra bit on page 96.)

To open the CSS panel, choose Window > CSS Styles or press [Ctrl][F11] (Windows) or [⌘][F11] (Mac).

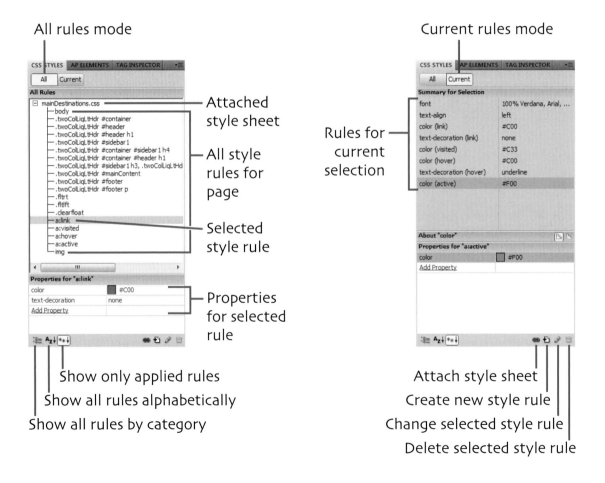

All rules mode

Current rules mode

Attached style sheet

All style rules for page

Selected style rule

Properties for selected rule

Rules for current selection

Show only applied rules
Show all rules alphabetically
Show all rules by category

Attach style sheet
Create new style rule
Change selected style rule
Delete selected style rule

Use the drop-down menu at the top right of the CSS panel group for such common tasks as duplicating a style rule or expanding and closing the group.

using the properties panel

In previous versions of Dreamweaver, using the Properties panel to create CSS often generated a mess of confusing, unnecessary styles. For that reason, we avoided using the Properties panel for any CSS work. The new version of the Properties panel, however, makes it clear when you are generating HTML or CSS code. Unlike previous versions, it also keeps you from accidentally creating a brand-new CSS rule every time you simply want to change an existing CSS rule. So now you have a real choice if you prefer to use the Properties panel instead of the CSS Styles tab.

1 To open the Properties panel, choose Window > Properties or press Ctrl F3 (Windows) or ⌘ F3 (Mac).

2 To create a new CSS rule, click the CSS button in the Properties panel, and choose < New CSS Rule > in the Targeted Rule drop-down menu.

3 Now click Edit Rule and a New CSS Rule dialog appears where you can define the new rule.

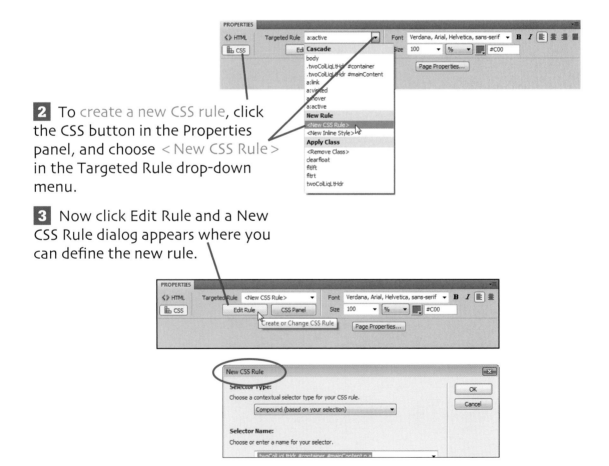

4 To change an existing CSS rule, first click on the item you want to change.

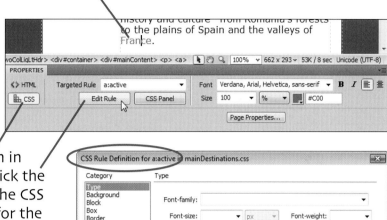

5 Click the CSS button in the Properties panel, click the Edit Rule button, and the CSS Rule Definition dialog for the existing rule appears. You can then change the rule as needed.

detach, attach style sheets

From the beginning of this book, we've been using pages already attached to a style sheet (mainDestinations.css in our examples). Let's detach a style sheet from a page to see how different unattached pages look, and then reattach it.

1 Make sure the CSS Styles tab is visible (Windows > CSS Styles) with the All button selected. Open your page (index.html in our example).

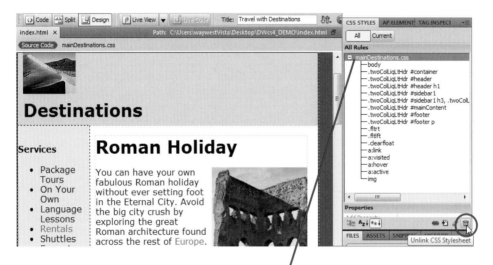

2 Select the style sheet in the CSS Styles tab (mainDestinations.css in our example) and click the Delete button at the bottom (the Trash can).

3 The style sheet is no longer listed in the CSS Styles tab (don't worry, it still exists), and the page loses most of its formatting. This simple top-to-bottom stacking of elements is called the page's natural flow since there's no style sheet to float items to the left or right.

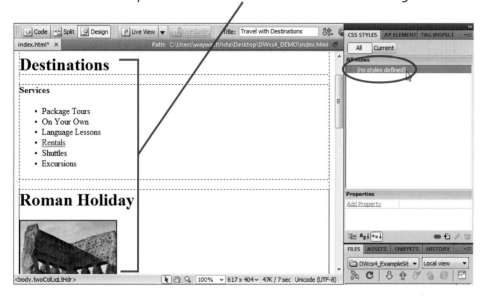

4 Let's reattach the previous style sheet. This process is the same one you'd use to change the look by attaching another style sheet instead. Start by clicking the chain-link Attach button in the CSS Styles tab.

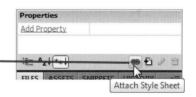

5 Click Browse to navigate to where the desired style sheet resides. (In our example, it's mainDestinations.css at the site's top level.) Make sure Link is selected and click OK. The page changes to reflect the style sheet's formatting, which in this example is exactly what we started with in step 1.

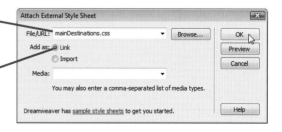

use style sheets

create a tag-based style

Tag-based styles affect every instance of a selected HTML element. Create a list style, for example, and it's applied to every list tag in every page attached to that style sheet.

1 Open your page (index.html in our example). Select the text in any list (not the list's heading however). Right-click (Option-click for single-button Macs) and choose CSS Styles > New in the context menu. (Or click the Add CSS Rule button (the plus) at the bottom of the CSS Styles tab. You also can use the Properties panel as explained in step 2 on page 80.)

2 In the New CSS Rule dialog, change the Selector Type to Tag.

3 Choose li (for list) in the Selector Name pop-up menu.

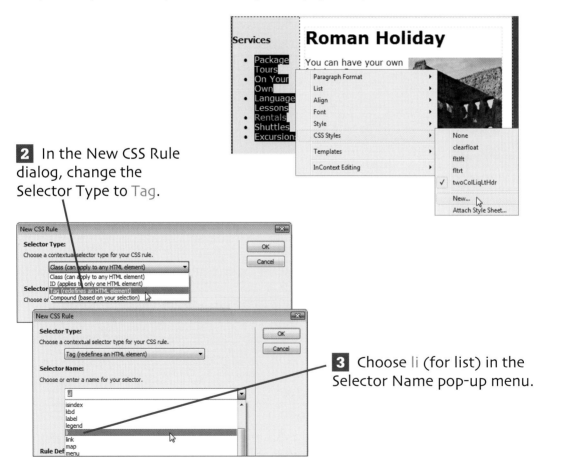

4 By default, the Rule Definition uses the page's external style sheet if there is one (mainDestinations.css in our example). Click OK to close the dialog.

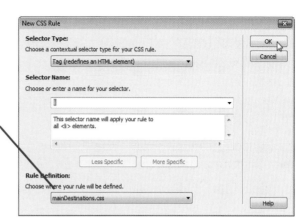

5 When the CSS Rule Definition dialog opens, the Type category is automatically selected. Set the Font-size and Color. (In our example, small and #666, a gray, are chosen to keep the list from competing visually with the page's main content.)

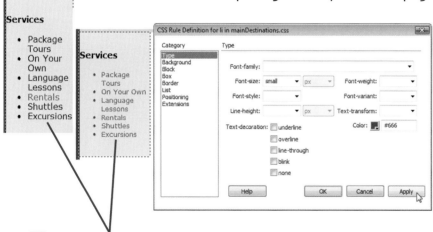

6 Click Apply to see the effect of the change. Adjust if necessary, then click OK to close the dialog.

7 Choose File > Save All and the new style for lists is applied to every list linked to that external style sheet.

use style sheets

create a compound style

You're not limited to applying tag-based styles to every instance of an HTML element. You also can define such styles so that they're applied only when a particular combination of elements appear in a specific part, or division, of a page. These compound (or context-based) styles are particularly powerful when used with Dreamweaver's predesigned layouts, which use div tags to mark the page's different divisions.

1 Make sure the CSS Styles tab is visible, and open your page (index.html in our example). Select the heading for the list used in the previous steps (Services in our example's sidebar list).

2 Right-click ([Option]-click for single- button Macs) and choose CSS Styles > New in the context menu. (Or click the Add CSS Rule plus button at the bottom of the CSS Styles tab. You also can use the Properties panel as explained in step 2 on page 80.)

3 In the New CSS Rule dialog, change the Selector Type to Compound. Let's look at what's inside the two Selector Name text windows. In our example, the first window reads: .twoColLiqLtHdr #container #sidebar1 h4. Below it, in the second window, each part of that of code is listed from most to least specific. The first bit of code, (a) .twoColLiqLtHdr, refers to the layout you first chose on page 12, which uses a two- column liquid layout with a header. The # leading off the next two bits of code (b, c) tells you these are page divisions marked with specific ID tags: container and sidebar1. Every CSS layout includes a #container. The #sidebar1 marks the sidebar holding the Services heading, which as the final bit of code (d) tells us is styled as an h4 (Heading 4). (See the first "create a compound style" extra bit on page 96.)

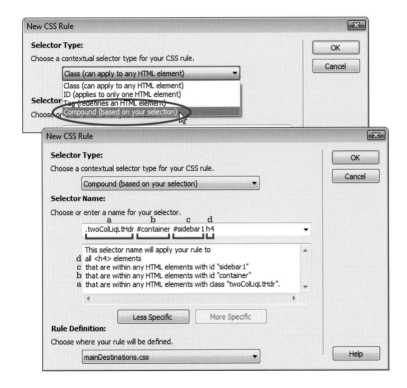

Here's the cool part about all this: because of what was selected in step 1, Dreamweaver has automatically identified Heading 4's context. All you have to do is choose Compound as the Selector Type and click OK. (See the second "create a compound-based style" extra bit on page 96.)

compound style (cont.)

4 In the CSS Rule Definition dialog that appears, use the left-side categories to precisely define how the selected element should look in this particular context. (In our example, we use the Type category to set the color to #666 to match the list color, and the Block category to set the heading alignment to center.)

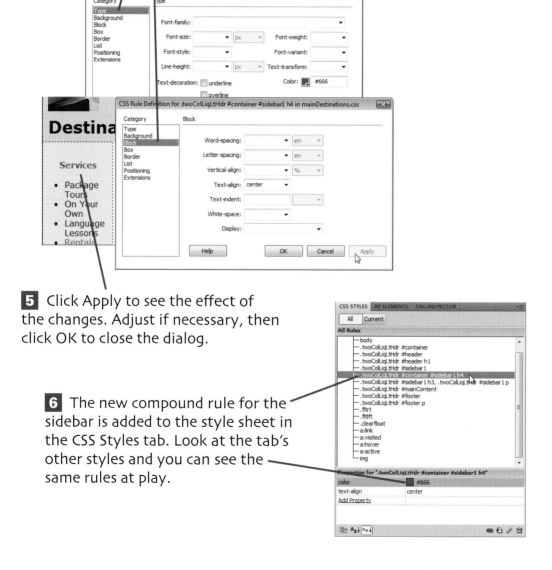

5 Click Apply to see the effect of the changes. Adjust if necessary, then click OK to close the dialog.

6 The new compound rule for the sidebar is added to the style sheet in the CSS Styles tab. Look at the tab's other styles and you can see the same rules at play.

7 Let's use compound styles to quickly make some other needed changes to our example. Click in the header's Heading 1 (Destinations). Right-click and choose CSS Styles > New in the context menu.

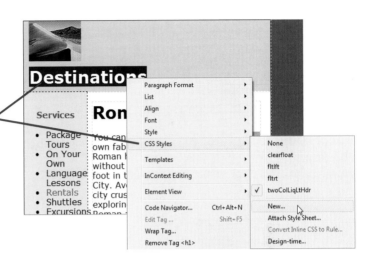

8 In the New CSS Rule dialog, change the Selector Type to Compound. Dreamweaver automatically generates a Selector Name based on the Heading 1, so click OK.

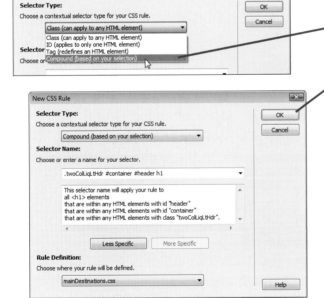

compound style (cont.)

9 In the Type category, set the Font-family to the Georgia, Times New Roman, Times, serif, the Font-size to xx-large, and the Color to #C00. Click Apply to see the effect of the change, and click OK to close the dialog.

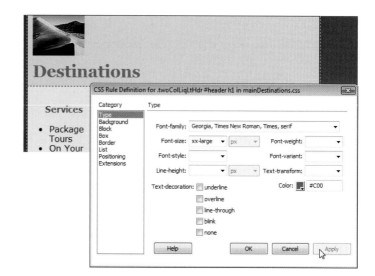

10 Let's make two more changes involving the header. Select the header's logo image (dunelogo100.jpg in our example). In the Properties panel set its alignment to Left.

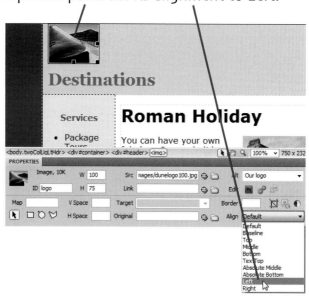

11 Click anywhere in the header, then click < div # header > in the status bar to select all of the header.

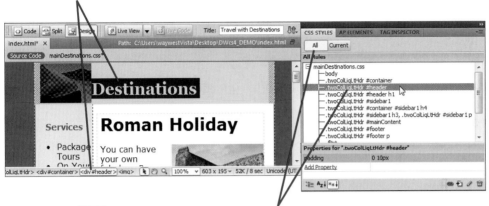

12 Leave the CSS Styles tab set to All and double-click the .twoColLiqLtHdr # header rule.

13 In the Background category, click the Background color drop-down menu and use the eye dropper that appears to select a color you'd like to use for the header's background (# 09F in our example).

use style sheets **91**

compound style (cont.)

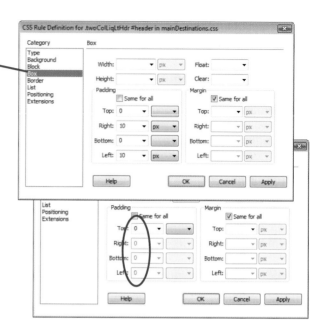

14 Now select the Box category and change all the Padding values to 0 (zero). Click OK to close the rule definition dialog.

15 Choose File > Save All to save your changes to the page and the attached style sheet. Click the Globe button in the Document toolbar to preview the changes in your default Web browser.

use style sheets

create class-based style

Class-based styles can be applied to multiple items on a page. In our example, we create a style for formatting quotes by customers. But class-based styles are also handy for such things as applying the same color to various elements to give your site a unified look.

1 Open any page to which you've already attached your main css style sheet. (In our example, we're still using index.html, which is attached to mainDestinations.css.) In the CSS Styles tab, click the Add CSS Rule button at the bottom of the tab. (You also can use the Properties panel as explained in step 2 on page 80.)

2 In the New CSS Rule dialog, select Class as the Selector Type. In the Selector Name text window, type pullquote and click OK to close the dialog.

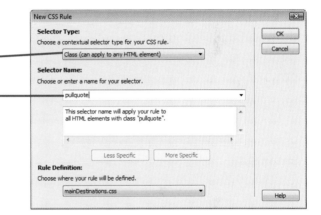

3 Use the various categories in the rule definition dialog to define the look of your pull quote. (In our example, we use the Type category to set the Font-family to Verdana, Geneva, sans-serif, the Font-size to small, the Font-weight to 200, the Font-style to italic, and the Color to #09F to match the header's new color.)

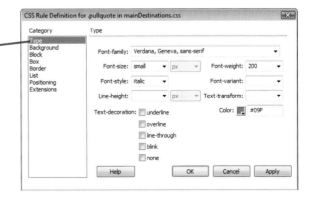

use style sheets

class-based style (cont.)

4 In our example, we use the Block category to make just one change: setting Text-align to right.

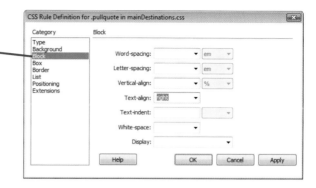

5 In our example, we use the Box category to set the Width to 250 (pixels), the Clear to both, and the Margin to 15 (pixels) all the way around.

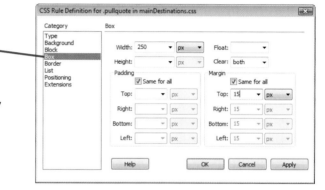

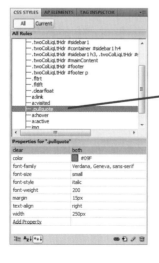

6 Click OK to close the dialog. The new rule appears in the CSS Styles tab with the properties you assigned.

use style sheets

7 To apply the new class-based rule, select the text you want formatted as a pull quote. (In our example, we have added a quote just above the Getting Around heading.) Right-click ([Option]-click for single-button Macs) the text, and choose CSS Styles > pullquote in the context menu.

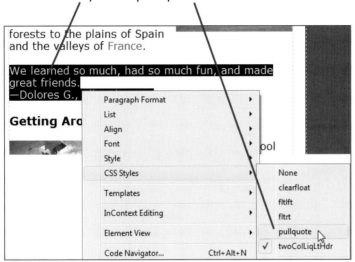

8 Click anywhere in the page to see the effect. Choose File > Save All to save the page and the style sheet.

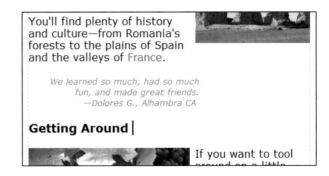

extra bits

using the css styles tab p. 78

- By default, the AP Elements and Tag Inspector tabs are grouped with the CSS Styles tab in the CSS panel group. The first controls absolutely positioned layout elements, while the second is used for hand coding. Neither tab is covered in this book.

create a compound style p. 86

- When creating a compound heading, don't undermine the relative sizing inherent in headings where heading 1 is the largest and heading 6 the smallest. For example, it makes sense to set a heading 1 to xx-large since it's the largest size available. But it would be potentially confusing to set a heading 1 to xx-small since there'd be nothing smaller available for headings 2–6.

- Another common use of a compound style might involve selecting a heading inside a table and creating a style that would apply only to that size heading in tables.

7. add interactivity

One of the great advantages of Web pages over printed pages is their ability to respond to viewers' actions. When used with restraint, this interactivity can entice your visitors to explore your site more thoroughly. Whether it's building a menu that responds to cursor movements or simply creating a form for collecting information from visitors, Dreamweaver's tools make it easy.

add navigation menu

Dreamweaver CS4 includes a set of tools called Spry widgets. Combining JavaScript and CSS, most of these widgets fall well beyond the scope of this beginner book. But one, the Spry Menu Bar, helps you create fly-out menus even if you're not a big-league code jockey.

1 Open your home page (index.html in our example) and click the Split view button.

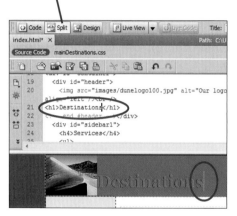
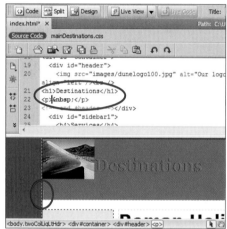

2 Looking at the header in the Code window, click after the heading (Destinations in our example) and press [Enter] (Windows) or [Return] (Mac) to give yourself some space to insert the navigation menu. Click the Design view button to switch out of the Split view.

3 Make sure the Spry tab is selected in the Insert toolbar/panel, then click the Spry Menu Bar button. Select the Horizontal button and click OK. (See the first "add navigation menu" extra bit on page 112.)

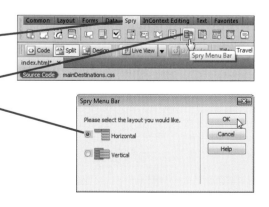

add interactivity

4 When the menu bar appears in the header, replace each label by selecting it inside the Properties panel's Text window, typing a new name, and pressing Tab. (In our example, the first items are replaced by Home and Where to Go.) (See the second "add navigation menu" extra bit on page 112.)

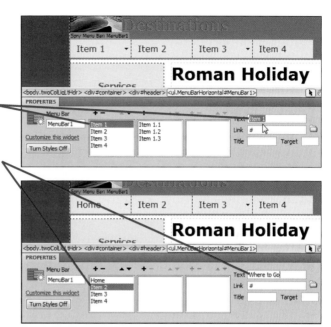

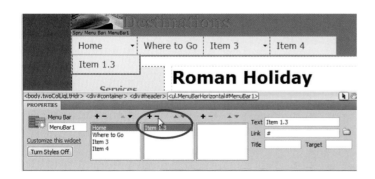

5 Use the Properties panel's plus and minus buttons to add or delete items at each level of the list. (In our example, all Home subitems are being removed, while subitems are being added to Where to Go.)

add interactivity

add navigation menu (cont.)

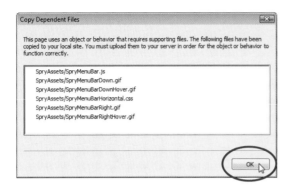

6 Choose File > Save All and click OK when Dreamweaver asks to copy a series of script and image files to your site.

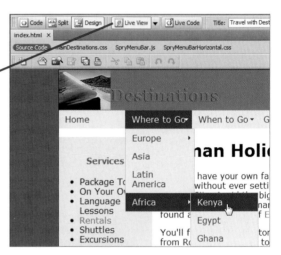

7 Click the Live View button in the Document toolbar to preview the changes and test the navigation menu without having to switch to a Web browser. Click the Live View button again to return to Dreamweaver's Design view where, if necessary, you can edit the menu labels.

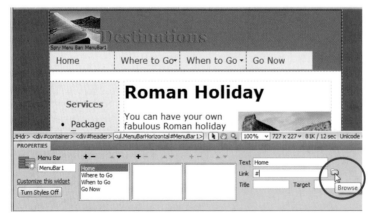

8 To link a label to its target page, select it in the menu and use the Properties panel's Link/Browse button to navigate to the page you want. Repeat to link all your navigation bar labels to their respective pages (or do this later after you create those pages).

add interactivity

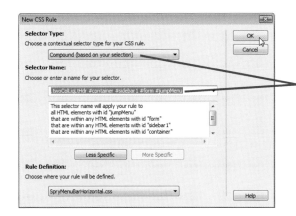

7 In the New CSS Rule dialog, the Selector Type is set automatically to Compound and a Selector Name for the jump menu is created as well. Simply click OK to begin defining the rule.

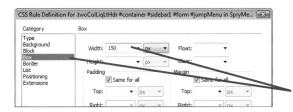

8 Based on what you learned in Chapter 6 about CSS, you can build as detailed a rule as you like. Be sure, at least, to use the Box category to define the jump menu's width so that it fits within the sidebar. Using the Type category to choose small also helps squeeze the jumpbar text into the sidebar's width.

9 When you finish defining the rule, click OK to close the definition dialog and your restyled menu appears with its new formatting.

10 Choose File > Save All. Click the Live View button in the Document toolbar to preview the changes in your default Web browser.

create form

Forms enable you to collect information from your visitors using simple text areas and buttons. As mentioned on page 63, they also offer you a way to receive messages from visitors without posting an email address on the Web site that gets grabbed by Web-crawling spammers. Before starting, check with the administrator for your Internet Service Provider or Web site to find out which System CGI (Get or Post) to use in step 5.

1 Create a new page for your site by duplicating the one you've been using and renaming it (form.html in our example). Replace the main content area with heading and text explaining the form.

2 Switch the Insert toolbar/panel to the Forms tab. Click the Form button. A blank form with a red dashed border appears on the page.

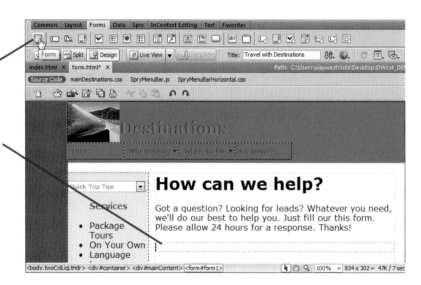

3 Select and cut your header and intro- ductory text, then paste it inside the red border, which sits within the yellow dashed border. Press [Enter] (Windows) or [Return] (Mac) to start a new paragraph.

How can we help?

Got a question? Looking for leads? Whatever you need, we'll do our best to help you. Just fill our this form. Please allow 24 hours for a response. Thanks!

4 In the Properties panel, replace the generic name assigned to the form with something that indicates its purpose.

5 From the Method drop-down menu, select the System CGI recommended for your Web server (POST in our example).

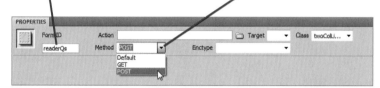

6 Click in the form where you want your first field to appear and click the Text Field button in the Forms tab.

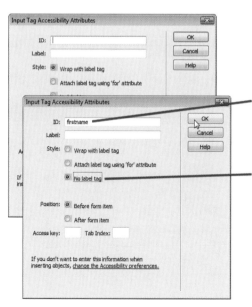

7 The Input Tag Accessibility Attributes dialog appears each time you use the Text Field button. Type in an ID that helps you recognize this field's purpose (firstname in our example since that's what it will hold). Don't use blank spaces or special characters since the ID is used in scripts, which don't recognize such characters. Select No label tag for a cleaner look, as explained in the next step. Click OK to close the dialog.

add interactivity

create form (cont.)

8 The new field is blank when it first appears in the form. In the Properties panel, use the Char width and Init val text windows to adjust the field's width and create an initial value that appears as a defacto label *inside* the field.

9 Repeat steps 6–8 for each text field you want added to the form.

10 To create a large text field for comments, click the Textarea button in the Forms tab. Create an ID when the Input Tag Accessibility Attributes dialog appears, and click OK to close the dialog.

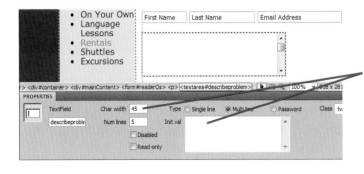

11 When the larger field appears in your form, use the Properties panel to set its width and initial value.

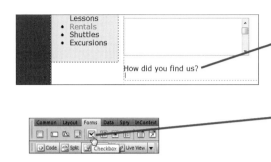

12 To create a multiple-choice question for readers, type the question below the previous text area. Press ⇧Shift Enter (Windows) or ⇧Shift Return (Mac) to start a new line and click the Checkbox button in the Forms tab. (See the "create form" extra bit on page 112.)

13 Create an ID in the Input Tag Accessibility Attributes dialog. In this case, create a label and select the After form item position. Since this form uses a checkbox, there's no room to tuck the label inside it. Click OK.

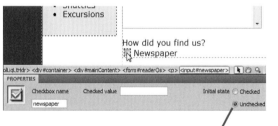

14 When the checkbox and label appear, check the Properties panel to make sure that its Initial state is set to Unchecked.

15 Repeat steps 12–14 until you create all the choices for the question.

add interactivity

create form (cont.)

16 To create a single-choice question for readers, type the question in the form. Press ⇧Shift Enter (Windows) or ⇧Shift Return (Mac) to start a new line and click the Radio Group button in the Forms tab.

17 Give the Radio Group a distinctive Name and rename each button using the Label column. If you need more items, click the ⊕ button. Click OK when you're done.

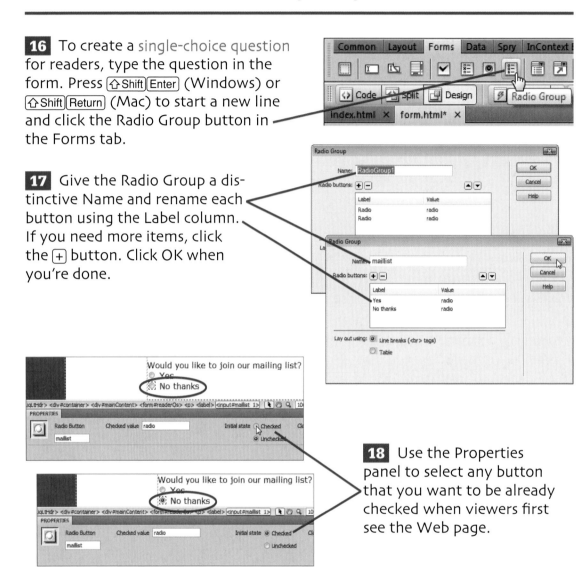

18 Use the Properties panel to select any button that you want to be already checked when viewers first see the Web page.

19 To give users a way to send in their responses, click the Button button in the Forms tab.

20 Create an ID when the Input Tag Accessibility Attributes dialog appears, and click OK to close the dialog.

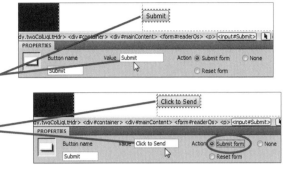

21 The new button is named Submit when it first appears in the form. Use the Value window to create a more helpful label (Click to Send in our example). By default, the Action is set to Submit form.

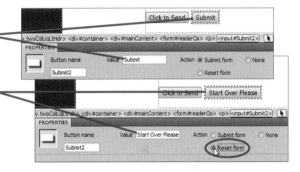

22 Repeat steps 19–21 to give users a second button to start over with the form. Again, use the Properties panel's Value window to relabel the button (Start Over Please in our example). Be sure to change the Action to Reset form.

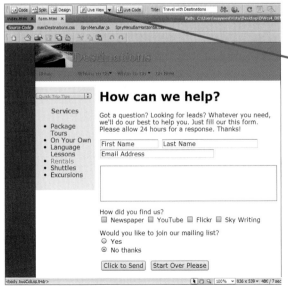

23 Choose File > Save All. Click the Live View button in the Document toolbar to preview the changes in your default Web browser. If necessary, click the Live View button again to return to the Design view where you can use the CSS Styles tab to format the form to reflect your Web site's overall look and design.

add interactivity   **111**

extra bits

add navigation menu p. 98

- In step 3, if you choose Vertical instead of Horizontal, all the rules in steps 9–14 are listed as MenuBarVertical... instead of MenuBarHorizontal.... Otherwise, the rest of the steps are the same.

- In step 4, while you can select and replace a menu label inside the document (instead of in the Properties panel's text window), it's easy to mess up your code. Another hazard of not using the Properties panel is that it will switch to something other than the Menu Bar with a single misclick. So stick with using the Properties panel's Text window for any label work.

- In step 14, the background color for the hover state was left the same, though you can change it if you want the rollover response to be more dramatic.

add jump menu p. 103

- In step 2, you also can choose Insert > Form > Jump Menu.

create form p. 106

- Use checkboxes when you want users to be able to pick more than one choice. Use radio buttons when you want users to pick just a single item.

add interactivity

8. reuse items to save time

Think of the Assets tab in the Files panel group as Dreamweaver's grand central timesaver. It automatically lists which images, color swatches, and external links you have used on your site. If you want to use those items again, the Assets tab makes it easy to quickly find what you need. For example, you can use the tab to build a list of favorite images, colors, or links. The Assets tab also includes library items, another major timesaver.

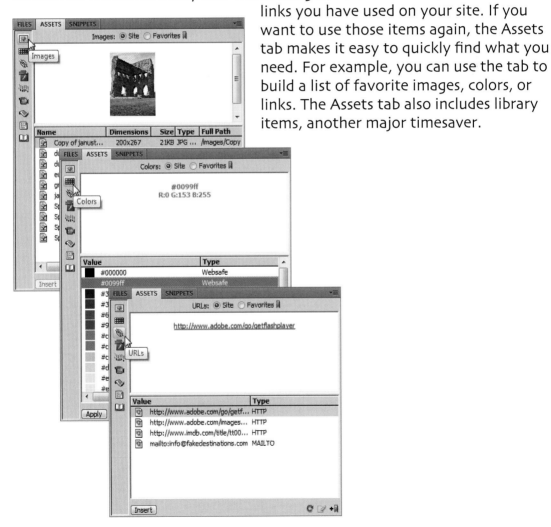

create a favorite

By creating favorites from the lists generated by the Assets tab, you always have your most-used items handy.

1 Choose Window > Assets to open the Assets tab and make sure the Site radio button is selected.

2 Select a category button in the left-hand column. (In our example, we've chosen the Images button at the top of the column because with so many images used, creating a shorter favorites list is essential.)

3 Select the image file you want to mark as a favorite.

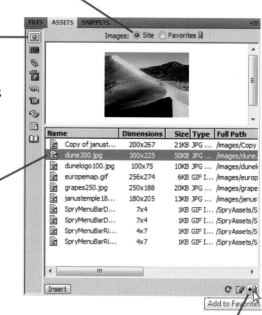

4 Click the Add to Favorites button at the bottom.

5 The first time you add a favorite, Dreamweaver displays a reminder dialog telling you how to see your favorites. To keep it from appearing each and every time you add a favorite, check Don't show me this message again and click OK. The image you marked is added to the list of favorite images.

use a favorite

With a favorites list, you save yourself from constantly digging through your Files tab.

1 Choose Window > Assets to open the Assets tab and click the Favorites radio button, and select a left-hand category button.

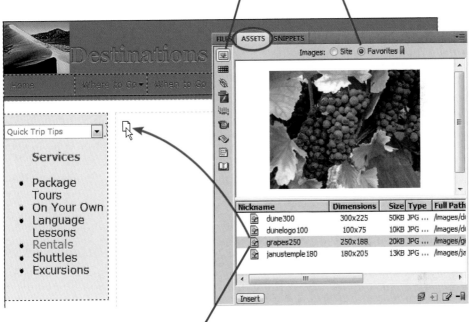

2 Select an image in the favorites list and drag it onto the page where you want it to appear.

create a library item

Make library items of anything you use repeatedly. It can be something simple like a 2 x 400-pixel rule. Or it can be as elaborate as the contents of a header. Short or long, the real benefit of a library item comes when you need to make a change—change it once and all pages using it automatically update.

1 Select the Library category button in the Assets tab of the Files panel.

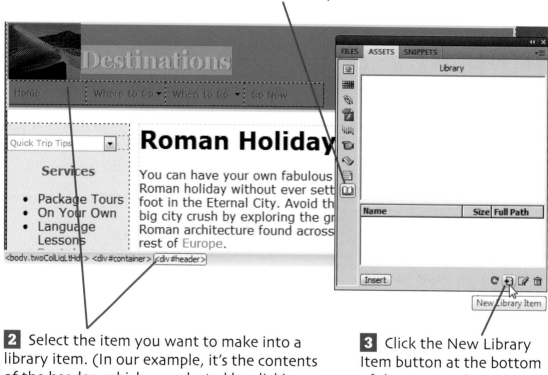

2 Select the item you want to make into a library item. (In our example, it's the contents of the header, which we selected by clicking < div # header > in the status bar.)

3 Click the New Library Item button at the bottom of the Assets tab.

reuse items to save time

4 Click OK when Dreamweaver warns that the library item cannot include the styling from the original page. However, leave Don't warn me again unchecked because you want to be reminded that this library item always needs to be reconnected to the original style sheet. (See the first "create library item" extra bit on page 120.)

5 A preview of the new library item (without the CSS formatting) appears in the top half of the Assets tab.

6 The still untitled file will be selected automatically in the bottom half of the tab.

7 Give the new library item a distinctive name and press ⌷Tab⌷ to apply it. (See the second "create library item" extra bit on page 120.)

8 Click Update when Dreamweaver asks to update its links.

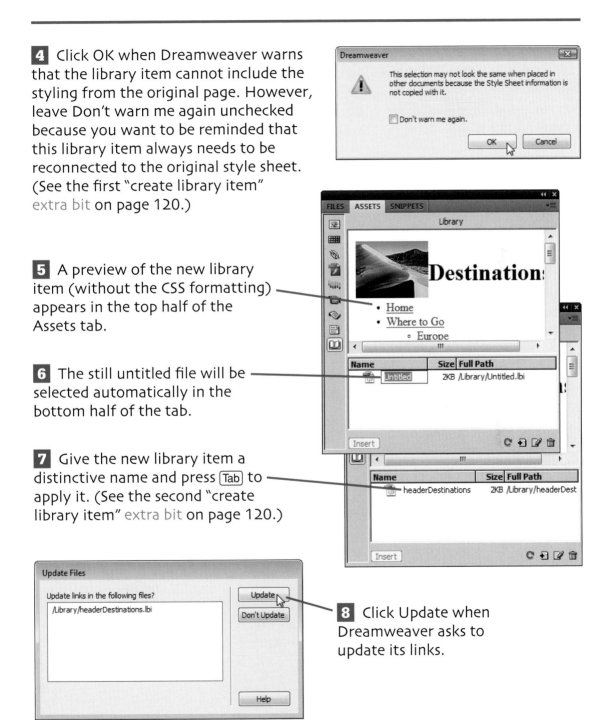

edit library item

In this example, we want to change the copyright notice. However, you can use this same process to update any library item—and all the pages using that item.

1 To fix it, click the Edit button at the bottom of the Assets tab.

2 When the library item appears, make your correction.

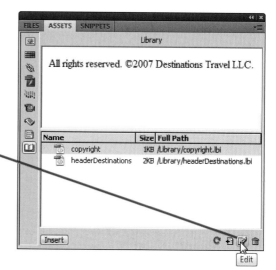

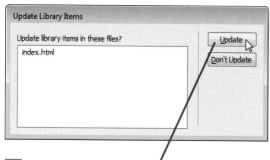

3 Save the changes and when Dreamweaver asks if it should change any pages containing this library item, click Update. When a second dialog appears listing which pages were updated, click Close.

The Assets tab's preview of the library item updates to reflect the changes. Close the edited library page to get it out of your way.

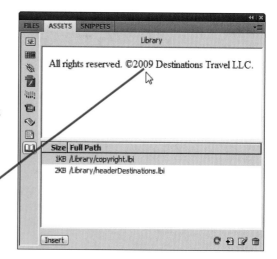

reuse items to save time

insert library item

Inserting a library item works similarly to adding a favorite to a page.

1 With the Assets tab of the Files panel open and visible, click in the open page where you want to place the selected library item or select an item you want replaced by the library item.

`<body.twoColLiqLtHdr> <div#container> <div#footer> <p>`   100% 834 x 432

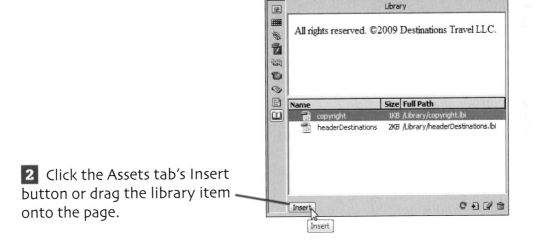

2 Click the Assets tab's Insert button or drag the library item onto the page.

`<body.twoColLiqLtHdr> <div#container> <div#footer> <mm:libitem>`   100% 834 x 432

3 The change is applied to the page.

extra bits

create a library item p. 116

- While library items contain no styling themselves, they can contain references to style sheets. Use external style sheets to keep library items consistently styled, as explained in Chapter 6.

- Dreamweaver automatically adds the .lbi suffix to a library item file name, designating the file as a library item.

reuse items to save time

9. publish site

Finally, you're ready to put your pages on the Web, a process sometimes called publishing since they'll become available for anyone to read. Dreamweaver's expanded Files tab displays files on the remote Web server, along with those on your local machine. It plays a key role in helping you keep track of which files are where and when they were last changed.

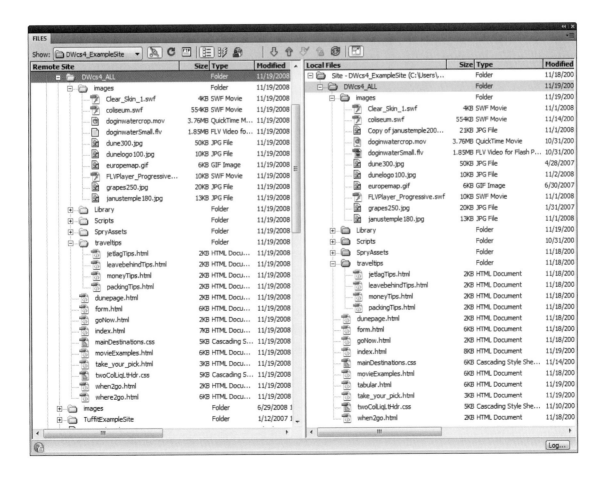

add search terms

It's easy for you to help Web search engines highlight your site if you enter a succinct description, along with multiple keywords, in the home page. Dreamweaver places this information in the page's hidden head code.

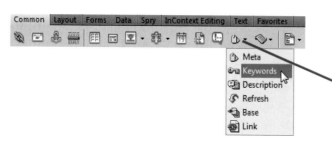

1 Open your home page and make sure the Common tab is selected in the Insert toolbar/panel. Click the button that looks like a luggage tag and choose Keywords from its drop-down menu.

2 When the Keywords dialog appears, type words that you think people might use to search for your site. Once you're done, click OK to close the dialog. (See the first "add search terms" extra bit on page 133.)

3 In the Common tab, click the same button which now looks like a key, reflecting your last choice, and choose Description from its drop-down menu.

4 When the Description dialog appears, type in a short paragraph that sums up the purpose of your Web site and the products it displays. Once you're done, click OK to close the dialog.

5 If you want to see the otherwise hidden keywords and description, click the Split button. The terms appear as part of the meta data in the page's head code. (See the second "add search terms" extra bit on page 133.)

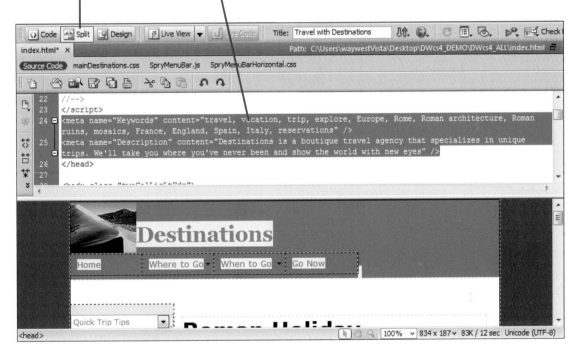

check and fix links

Few things are more frustrating for Web users than broken links. Dreamweaver can check your entire site in seconds and save everyone hours of frustration.

1 Choose Site > Check Links Sitewide. The Link Checker tab in the Results area lists any pages with broken links.

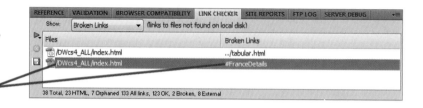

2 Double-click any file listed and Dreamweaver opens the Properties panel, along with the page that contains the broken link.

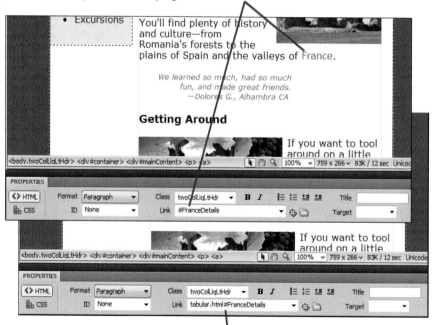

3 Use the Properties panel's Link text field to correct the mistake by typing in the correct link or redrawing the link with the Point to File button.

4 Once you make the fix, save the page and the Results panel automatically removes the broken link from its list. Repeat until you've fixed all broken links.

explore the files panel

The Files panel serves as your main tool to put files from your local site on to the Web server that will host your files, known as the remote site. You also use it to get any of your remote files if, for example, you've accidentally deleted their local site counterparts.

Normally the Files panel only shows your local files. Click the Expand/Collapse button to see them along with your remote Web site's files.

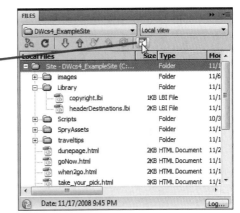

The toolbar running above the file listings contains all the buttons needed to move files between the two locations.

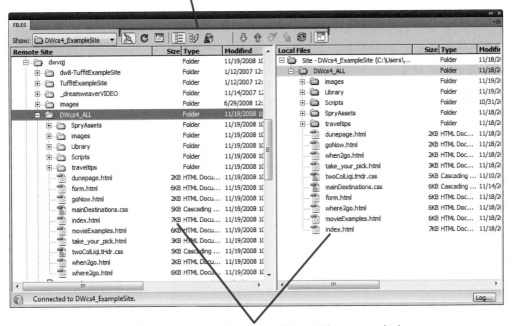

The expanded view of the Files panel shows your remote and local files. (See the first "explore the files panel" extra bit on page 133.)

explore the files panel (cont.)

Click the
Connect/Disconnect
button to open or close
a live connection to the
remote Web site.

Click the Get files
button to move
selected files from
the remote site to
the local site.

Click the Put files
button to move
selected files from
your local site to
the remote site.

Show: DWcs4_ExampleSite

Click the Refresh
button after moving
files in either direc-
tion to update the
file listings.

Do not use these two buttons
unless you're working with a
group of people and have acti-
vated Dreamweaver's check-in/
check-out file system. (See the
second "explore the files panel"
extra bit on page 133.)

The Expand/Collapse button
lets you see the remote and
local files, or just the local files.

set up remote site

After double-checking your files, you're ready to add the details about the remote site. Your computer is the local site, whose details you defined on page 8. (See the first two "set up remote site" extra bits on page 133.)

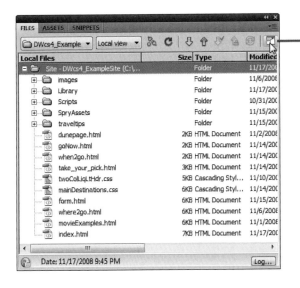

1 In the Files tab, click the Expand/Collapse button.

2 In the Remote Site panel, click the link labeled "define a remote site".

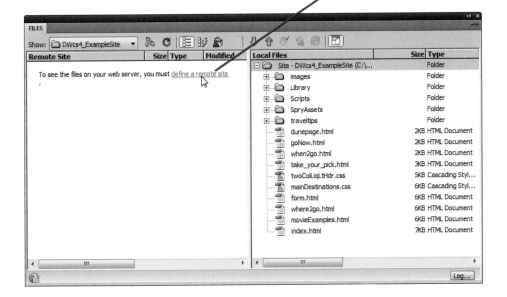

set up remote site (cont.)

3 The Advanced view appears in the Site Definition dialog with the Remote Info category automatically selected. Choose FTP in the Access drop-down menu.

4 Fill in the FTP address for your new site, based on information provided by the firm hosting your site.

5 You don't have to specify a Host directory (the folder on the remote site that will contain the site), but you can create one if it helps keep your site better organized.

6 Fill in your login and password, again based on the information from your Web host.

7 Select Use passive FTP unless your Web host firm specifically tells you not to do so.

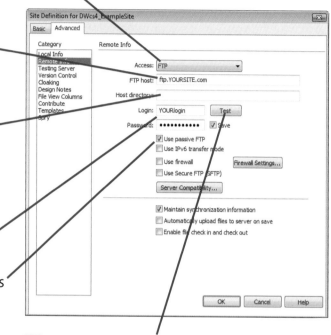

8 Assuming you're already online, click Test and it will take only a moment for Dreamweaver to determine if the connection is working.

9 If the test connection works, click OK to close the message dialog. Close the Site Definition dialog by clicking OK. (See the last "set up remote site" extra bit on page 133.)

publish site

connect to remote site

Having set up the remote site, you're ready to connect to it.

1 Make sure you are connected to the Internet.

2 Return to Dreamweaver, make sure the Files panel is visible, and click the Expand/Collapse button.

3 Once the view expands, click the Connect button.

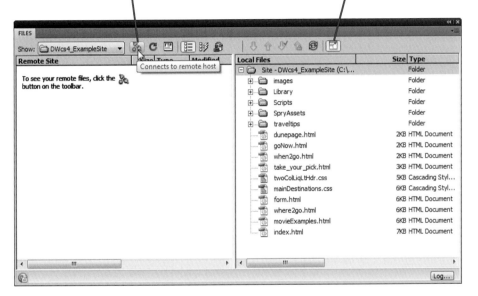

4 The status dialog appears briefly as Dreamweaver negotiates the connection to your Web site.

5 Once the connection is made, the remote site's files appear in the left side of the Files panel.

6 You're ready to upload your files.

upload multiple files

If this is the first upload to your Web site, you'll be publishing multiple files, including all the necessary images for your pages.

1 In the Local Files panel, click to select the top-level folder that contains all the files you want to upload (DWcs4_ALL in our example).

You also can select individual files or folders by Ctrl-clicking (Windows) or ⌘-clicking (Mac) them in the Local Files panel.

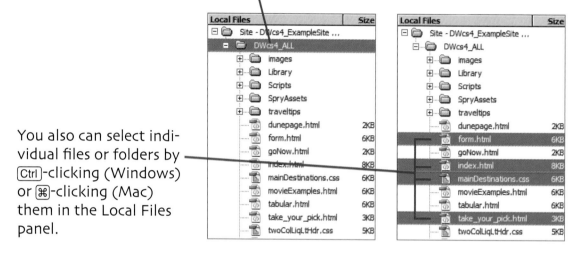

2 Drag the selected local files to the folder in the Remote Site panel or click the Put button to upload them. (See the "upload multiple files" extra bit on page 133.)

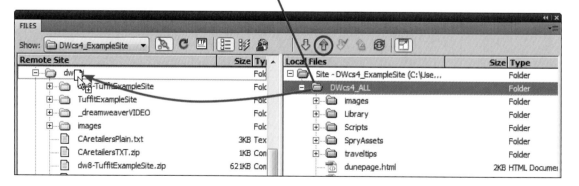

3 Click Yes when Dreamweaver asks whether you want to upload dependent files for your pages, such as images.

This may take several minutes to complete, depending on how many files you're uploading and the speed of your Internet connection.

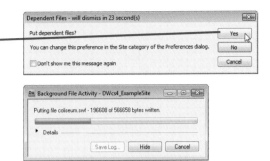

4 When the progress dialogs stop appearing, press the Refresh button...

5 ...and then compare names of the Remote Site files to the names of your Local Files.

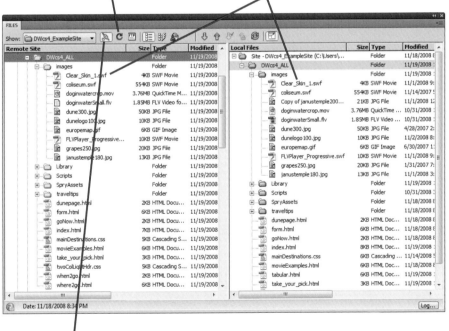

6 Check how the remote site pages look in your Web browser to make sure their appearance matches that of your local files. If you find mismatches, upload the local files again.

7 Once you're done, click the Disconnect button.

publish site

upload a single page

Sometimes you'll need to upload only a single page—for example, when you need to update information or fix a mistake.

1 Once you're connected, click the page file in the Local Files panel and drag it to the folder where the older version appears in the Remote Site panel.

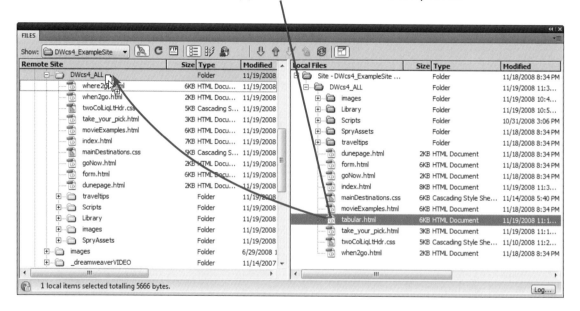

2 A single progress dialog appears as Dreamweaver uploads the selected page. Use your Web browser to check the page on the remote Web site, and when you're done, click the Disconnect button.

extra bits

add search terms p. 122

- When picking keywords and a description, especially for an uncommon product or service, think of similar products or services and use words people would most likely type in to find them.

- You can add keywords or descriptive terms any time by clicking the respective icon in the Common tab. While the dialog will be blank, any words you entered earlier are still there in the header. To see and remove words, you have to do it manually using Split view.

explore the files panel p. 125

- In the past, it could be tough to make room on even a large screen for a good view of your Web pages and the full Files panel. Dreamweaver CS4 solves that problem by enabling you to quickly switch between the expanded and icon views of the Files panel (see page 5).

- If you are working solo, the check-in/check-out system is cumbersome since it forces you to alert yourself that you're using a file. If, however, you're working solo and using multiple computers, say a desktop and a laptop, the checkout system helps keep all the files in synch.

set up remote site p. 127

- Check ahead with your Web site host to get the information needed for the Remote Info category. The great majority of sites use FTP to access sites, but asking ahead never hurts.

- Web-hosting firms usually email you a login name and password for posting your files. Keep the original email where you won't delete it and can find it later. If you ever buy a new computer, you'll need that password because Dreamweaver never reveals the password, just those black dots.

- If the test connection fails, double-check your entries in the Site Definition dialog. Note that entries are case sensitive. Almost inevitably, you'll find a mistyped entry.

upload multiple files p. 130

- In step 2 of our example, the DWcs4_ALL folder is dragged and dropped into my site's existing dwvqj folder. The other files visible in the dwvqj folder were created for this book's previous editions.

index

sign, 65, 75, 87

#container tag, 87

#sidebar tag, 87

2-column liquid layouts, 12, 87

A

a:active link state, 74

Access menu, Site Definition dialog, 128

Accessibility section, Table dialog, 46, 57

active link state, 70, 74

Add CSS Rule button, 84, 86, 93

Add to Favorites button, 114

addresses, linking to email, 63

Adobe

    Bridge, 2, 7

    Creative Suite 4, xiii, 4

    Dreamweaver CS4. See Dreamweaver CS4

    Fireworks, xiii, 25, 26

    Flash video, 29–31, 44

    Photoshop, xiii, 25, 26

    Photoshop Elements, xiii

Advanced tab, Site Definition dialog, 8, 128

a:hover link state, 74

Align Center button, 23

Align setting, Properties panel, 26, 90

a:link rule, 71

All rules mode, 78

Alt text window, Properties panel, 26, 44, 68

Alternate text, 18, 28, 44

anchor icon, 65

anchor links, 64–65, 75

AP Elements tab, 78, 96

Ascending sort order, 56

Assets tab, 113–119

    creating favorites with, 114

    creating library items with, 116–119

    Edit button, 118

    Insert button, 119

    purpose of, 6, 113

Attach button, 83

audio Web browsers, 44, 46, 57

a:visited link state, 74

B

background color, 91, 101, 102, 112

Basic tab, Site Definition dialog, 8

Blank Page option, 12, 24

Block category, CSS Rule Definition dialog, 88, 94

Border setting, Properties panel, 26

borders

    image, 71, 72, 73

    table, 46, 57

Box category, CSS Rule Definition dialog, 92, 94

Bridge, 2, 7

Bridge button, 7

Brightness/Contrast sliders, 36, 44

broken links, 124

browsers. See Web browsers

bulleted lists, 21, 22

Button button, Forms tab, 110

index

c

Cascading Style Sheets. See also CSS
    as alternative to table-based layouts, 45
    more advanced book on, 77
    and Properties panel, 80–81
    purpose of, viii, 77
cell labels, 46, 47
cell padding, 46, 53
cell spacing, 53
cells. See also tables
    adding, 47, 48
    aligning text in, 50–51
    inserting images into, 57
    labeling, 46, 47
    merging, 50
    selecting, 48
    splitting, 57
CGI methods, 106
chain-link icon, 83
check-in/check-out file system, 126, 133
Check Links Sitewide command, 124
checkboxes, 109, 112
class-based styles, 77, 93–95
Classic workspace, 4, 27, 29
Code view, 2
collapsing/expanding
    Insert toolbar, 3
    panels, 5, 6, 10
colors
    background, 91, 101, 102, 112
    building list of favorite, 113
    link, 70–74
    reusing, 113
    text, 85, 88, 90, 93, 101
columnar tables, 45. See also tables
columns
    adding, 47, 49

    aligning text in, 50–51
    labeling, 50
    setting width of, 46
    sorting data in, 55–56, 57
    zooming in on, 49
comma-delimited data, 57
Common tab
    adding keywords with, 122, 133
    adding site description with, 122
    Email Link button, 63
    Image button, 27
    key button, 122
    link-related buttons, 59
    luggage-tag button, 122
    Media button, 29, 32
    Named Anchor button, 64
    purpose of, 3
    Table button, 46
companion Web site, vii, xii
company logos, 17
compass-like icon. See Point to File icon
compound headings, 96
compound styles, 77, 86–92, 96
computer
    setting up local site on, 8–9, 10
    storing site's files on, 8
    text-size considerations, 24
Connect button, 126, 129
contact information, 23
container tags, 87
context-based styles, 77, 86, 104. See also
    compound styles
Contrast/Brightness sliders, 36, 44
copyright information, 23, 118
copyright symbol, 23
Create New File option, 12
creating
    basic Web site, 11–24

custom view setups, 7
favorites, 114
headings, 19–20, 24
home page, 12–14
image thumbnails, 37–39
library items, 116–119
lists, 21–22
style rules, 78, 80
Creative Suite 4, xiii, 4
Crop button, Properties panel, 34
cropping images, 34–35, 44
CS4 applications, 4. See also Creative Suite 4
CSS. See also Cascading Style Sheets
    code, 4, 10, 80
    identifying files supporting, 2
    meaning of acronym, 77
    and Spry widgets, 98
CSS button, 4, 23, 80, 81
CSS panel group, 78–79, 96
CSS Rule Definition dialog, 71, 81, 85, 88
CSS Styles tab
    attaching/detaching style sheets with, 82–83
    buttons/controls on, 78–79
    and class-based styles, 93–95
    and compound styles, 86, 88, 91
    purpose of, 6, 78
    using Properties panel instead of, 80
    wrapping text around images with, 42
Current rules mode, 78

D

Data tab, Insert toolbar, 52, 57
Delete button, CSS Styles tab, 82
Delimiter options, Import Tabular Data, 53
Descending sort order, 56
Description dialog, 122
Design view, 2, 10

Detect Size button, 30
Disconnect button, 126, 131, 132
div tags, 86
Document toolbar
    Globe button, 51, 54, 61, 69, 92
    Live View button. See Live View button
    view options, 2
double arrow, 5
Dreamweaver CS4
    buttons/controls, 2–7
    creating basic web site with, 11–24
    exploring, 2–7
    as image editor, 25
    launching, 8
    more advanced book on, xiv
    purpose of, vii
    what you can create with, viii–ix
Dreamweaver CS4 for Windows and Macintosh:
    Visual QuickStart Guide, xiv, 77
Dreamweaver Site button, 8

E

Edit > Rename command, 39
Edit button, 118
Edit Rule button, 81
Edit Rule command, 80
editing
    CSS rules, 80–81
    images, 25, 44
    library items, 118
element-based styles, 77
em-dashes, 16
Email Link button, 63
email links, 63
embedded video, 31
example files, vii, xii, 133
Excel spreadsheets, 52

index

Expand/Collapse button, 125, 126, 127, 129
expanding/collapsing
   Insert toolbar, 3
   panels, 5, 6, 10
external links, 59, 62, 75, 113
external style sheets, 85, 120
"extra bits" sections, xi
eye dropper, 91, 101

F

favorites, 113, 114–115
Favorites panel, 7
Favorites radio button, 115
File > New command, 12
File > Save command, 14
file names, 24
files
   checking in/out, 126, 133
   keeping in synch, 133
   keeping track of, 121
   moving between local/remote site, 125
   this book's example, vii, xii, 133
   updating, 126
   uploading to remote site, 130–132
   viewing local/remote, 125, 129
Files panel
   adding local site to, 9
   Assets tab. See Assets tab
   buttons/controls, 125–126
   and cropped images, 44
   Expand/Collapse button, 125, 126, 127, 129
   and image links, 66
   as main tool for putting files on remote site,
     125
   purpose of, 125
   Snippets tab, 6, 10
   switching between expanded and icon views
     of, 133

   and text links, 60
   viewing local/remote files in, 125, 129
Files panel group, 6, 113
Files tab, 14, 78, 121
Fireworks, xiii, 25, 26
Flash video, 29–31, 44
.fltlft rule, 43
.fltrt rule, 42–43
.flv files, 29, 44. See also Flash video
fly-out menus, 98
folder button, 8
Folders panel, 7
font families, 90, 93
font size, 85, 90, 93, 102
font style, 93
font weight, 93
footers, 23
Form button, 106
formatting
   footers, 23
   headers, 15
   menus, 101
   quotes, 93
   tables, 47, 48, 53, 54
forms, 106–111
   adding comment field to, 108
   adding multiple-choice questions to, 109
   adding single-choice questions to, 110
   adding Submit button to, 111
   adding text fields to, 107–108
   adding to Web page, 106
   checkboxes vs. radio buttons in, 112
   cutting and pasting text into, 107
   naming, 107
   previewing in Web browsers, 111
   purpose of, 106
   and System CGI methods, 106
Forms tab, Insert toolbar, 103, 106, 107

frames-based layouts, 24
FTP address, 128, 133

G

"Get files" button, 126
Get method, 106
Globe button, 51, 54, 61, 69, 92
graphics. See images
graphics programs, 25, 26, 34
grid, 2

H

<h1> tags, 17, 19
<h2> tags, 19
<h3> tags, 20
head code, 122, 123
Header section, Table dialog, 46
header tags, 17
headers
    aligning, 90
    choosing background color for, 91
    creating library item from, 116–117
    formatting, 15
headings
    creating, 19–20, 24
    relative sizing of, 96
    saving, 20
    size considerations, 24
hiding/showing
    Invisible Elements, 75
    Properties panel, 4
    toolbars, 3
home page
    adding footer to, 23
    adding images to, 27–28
    adding lists to, 21–22

    adding search terms to, 122–123
    adding table to, 46–47
    adding text to, 15–16
    creating, 12–14
    creating headings for, 19–20, 24
    naming, 14, 24
    saving, 14
horizontal alignment, in tables, 51
Horizontal button, Spry Menu Bar, 98, 112
horizontal rules, 44
Horz pop-up menu, 51
Host directory, 128
hot spots, 67–69, 75
hover link state, 70, 74, 102, 112
HTML button, 50, 54
HTML code, vii, 4, 10, 80
HTML page type, 12
.html suffix, 14
hyperlinks, 59. See also links

I

icon panel, 5
icons, collapsing panels into, 5, 10
ID tags, 87
image editors, xiii, 25
image links, 66
image maps, 26, 67–69, 75
image placeholders, 17–18, 40–41
image thumbnails. See thumbnails
image tools, Properties panel, 26, 44
images, 25–44
    adding to tables, 57
    adding to Web pages, 27–28
    adjusting contrast/brightness of, 36, 44
    building list of favorite, 113, 114–115
    creating thumbnails of, 37–39
    cropping, 34–35, 44

index

images (continued)

  enlarging, 44

  entering Alternate text for, 18, 28, 44

  finding, 7

  flowing text around, 42–43

  inserting placeholders for, 17–18

  jumping among most used, 7

  naming, 18, 44

  reducing, 38

  resampling, 38, 44

  reusing, 113

  saving, 28

  toggling between compact and big-screen view of, 7

  updating links to renamed, 39

  viewing size of, 26

  zooming in/out on, 7

Import Tabular Data button, 57

importing tabular data, 52–54

index.html file, 14, 24

Input Tag Accessibility Attributes dialog, 107, 108, 109

Insert button, 119

Insert Column button, 49

Insert command, 3

Insert FLV dialog, 29, 30

Insert panel, 3

Insert Row buttons, 47, 48, 51

Insert toolbar

  Common tab. See Common tab

  Data tab, 52, 57

  expanding/collapsing, 3

  Forms tab, 103, 106

  Layout tab, 3, 47, 49, 51

  showing/hiding, 3

interactivity, 97–112

  benefits of, 97

  with forms, 106–111, 112

  with jump menus, 103–105, 112

  with navigation menus, ix, 98–102, 112

internal links, 59, 60–61, 75

Invisible Elements, 75

item lists, ix

J

JavaScript, 2, 3, 44, 98

Jump Menu button, 103

Jump Menu command, 112

jump menus, ix, 103–105, 112

K

key button, 122

keywords, 122–123, 133

Keywords dialog, 122

L

labels

  button, 111

  checkbox, 109

  column, 50

  form field, 108

  menu, 99, 112

  navigation bar, 100

  table cell, 46, 47

laptop users, 10, 133

launching program, 8

layer-based layouts, 24

Layout tab, Insert toolbar, 3, 47, 49, 51

layouts

  frames-based, 24

  layer-based, 24

  liquid, 12, 87

  style-sheet-based, 24

table-based, 45
.lbi suffix, 120
library items, 116–120
   and Assets tab, 113, 116–119
   creating, 116–117
   editing, 118
   ensuring consistent styles for, 120
   examples of, ix, 116
   file suffix for, 120
   inserting, 119
   naming, 117
   previewing, 117
   purpose of, 116
   updating links to, 117
Link/Browse button, 100
Link Checker tab, 124
link states, 70, 74
Link text window, Properties panel, 26, 62, 65,
   66, 124
links, 59–75
   anchor, 64–65, 75
   building list of favorite, 113
   checking/fixing broken, 124
   email, 63
   image, 39, 66
   internal *vs.* external, 59
   removing underlines from, 72
   reusing, 113
   setting colors for, 70–74
   testing, 61, 62, 63, 69
   updating, 117
liquid layouts, 12, 87
list styles, 84
lists, 21–22
Live View button
   and Flash video, 31
   and forms, 111
   and jump menus, 105

and navigation menus, 100, 102
   purpose of, 2
Local Files panel, 130, 132
Local root folder, 8
local site
   moving files to/from, 126
   naming, 8, 10
   setting up, 8–9, 10
   viewing files for, 121
login/password information, 128, 133
luggage-tag button, 122

M

Macintosh, text-size considerations for, 24
Map field, Properties panel, 26
Media button, 29, 32
menus
   fly-out, 98
   jump, ix, 103–105, 112
   navigation, ix, 3, 98–102, 112
Merge Cells command, 50
meta data, 123
Method menu, Properties panel, 107
multiple-choice questions, 109

N

Named Anchor button, 64
Named Anchor dialog, 65
naming
   form fields, 107
   forms, 107
   home page, 14, 24
   image maps, 75
   images, 18, 44
   library items, 117
   local site, 8, 10

index

naming (continued)
  style sheets, 13, 24
natural flow, 83
navigation menus, 98–102
  adding/deleting items in, 99
  changing formatting of, 101
  choosing colors for, 101–102
  choosing font size for, 102
  creating, 98–99
  linking labels to target pages, 100
  previewing, 100, 102
  purpose of, ix
  and Spry widgets, 3, 98
  vertical vs. horizontal, 112
Negrino, Tom, xiv
New command, 12
New CSS Rule button, 70, 72
New CSS Rule dialog
  and class-based styles, 93
  and compound styles, 87, 89
  defining new rules in, 80
  and link colors, 70, 72
  Selector Name menu, 70, 80, 84, 87
  Selector Type options, 70, 72, 87, 89, 93
  and tag-based styles, 84
New Document dialog, 12
New Workspace command, 4
numbered lists, 21

O

Ordered List button, 21
ordered lists, 21

P

Padding values, 92
page titles, 12, 13, 24

panel stack, 6
panels. See also specific panels
  choosing arrangement of, 4
  expanding/collapsing, 5, 6, 10
passwords, 128, 133
PC, text size on Windows, 24
Photoshop, xiii, 25, 26
Photoshop Elements, xiii
pixels, 35, 44
placeholders
  image, 17–18, 40–41
  video, 30, 33
Plugin command, 32
Point to File icon, 40, 60, 66, 68
Post method, 106, 107
Preview check box, Sharpen dialog, 38
progress dialog, 131, 132
Progressive Download Video option, 30
Properties panel
  Align setting, 26, 90
  Alt text window, 26, 44, 68
  as alternative to CSS Styles tab, 80
  Border setting, 26
  context-sensitive nature of, 4
  Contrast/Brightness button, 36
  Crop button, 34
  CSS button, 4, 23, 80, 81
  and CSS work, 80–81
  Forms tab, 107, 108, 110
  Horz pop-up menu, 51
  HTML button, 50, 54
  image tools, 26, 44
  Link/Browse button, 100
  link-related buttons, 62
  Link text window, 26, 62, 65, 66, 124
  Map field, 26
  Method menu, 107
  and navigation menus, 99, 100, 112

opening, 80
Ordered List button, 21
Point to File icon, 40, 60, 66, 68
Resample button, 38, 44
Sharpen button, 38
showing/hiding, 4
Src window, 26, 33, 35
Target menu, 26, 62
Targeted Rule menu, 80
Unordered List button, 22
Value window, 111
Vert pop-up menu, 50
Property Inspector. See Properties panel
publishing, 121–133
   adding search terms prior to, 122–123
   checking/fixing links prior to, 124
   connecting to remote site, 129
   defined, 121
   multiple files, 130–131, 133
   role of Files panel in, 125–126
   setting up remote site, 127–128
   single page, 132
pull quotes, 95
"Put files" button, 126

Q

QuickTime video, 32–33
quotes, 93, 95

R

radio buttons, 110, 112
Radio Group button, 110
Refresh button, 126
Related Files toolbar, 13, 44
relative sizing, 96

remote site, 127–133
   checking in Web browser, 131
   connecting to, 129
   disconnecting from, 131, 132
   moving files to/from, 126
   opening/closing connection to, 126
   setting up, 127–128, 133
   testing connection to, 128, 133
   uploading files to, 130–132
   viewing files on, 121
Remote Site panel, 127, 130–131, 132
Rename command, 39
Resample button, 38, 44
resampling images, 38, 44
"Reset form" action, 111
root folder, 44
rows
   adding, 47, 48, 51
   selecting, 48
   setting height of, 46
Rule Definition section, New CSS Rule dialog,
   72, 85
ruler, 2
rules
   horizontal, 44
   style, 78–81

S

Save As dialog, 14
Save command, 14
saving
   headings, 20
   home page, 14
   images, 28
   menus, 102, 105
   style sheets, 13
   tables, 47, 51

index

saving (continued)
   videos, 30, 33
   workspaces, 4
screenshots, x
Scripts folder, 31
search engines, 122
search terms, 122–123, 133
Select Image Source dialog, 27
Selector Name menu, New CSS Rule dialog, 70, 72, 84, 87, 93
Selector Type options, New CSS Rule dialog, 70, 72, 87, 89, 93
Sharpen button, 38
showing/hiding
   Invisible Elements, 75
   Properties panel, 4
   toolbars, 3
sidebars, 20, 21, 87
single-choice questions, 110
Site > Check Links Sitewide command, 124
Site Definition dialog, 8–9, 10, 128, 133
site description, 122–123, 133
Skin styles, 30
Smith, Dori, xiv
Snippets tab, 6, 10
Sort Table command, 55
Sort Table dialog, 55–56, 57
spammers, 63, 106
special characters, 15, 16, 23, 24
Split Cell command, 57
Split Vertically command, 2
Split view, 2, 17, 18, 98, 133
spreadsheets, 52
Spry Menu Bar widget, 98
Spry widgets, 3, 98
Src window, Properties panel, 26, 33, 35
Standard toolbar, 2
Start Page, 8

status dialog, 129
style rules, 78–81
   changing, 81
   creating, 78, 80
   deleting, 78
   duplicating, 79
   viewing, 78
style-sheet-based layouts, 24
style sheets. See also Cascading Style Sheets; styles
   attaching/detaching, 82–83
   and library items, 120
   naming, 13, 24
   purpose of, 77
   saving, 13
   tools for creating/managing, 78–79
styles
   class-based, 77, 93–95
   compound, 77, 86–92, 96
   context-based, 77, 86, 104
   element-based, 77
   keeping track of, 6
   tag-based, 77, 84–85
   viewing details of currently selected, 6
Submit button, 111
"Submit form" action, 111
.swf files, 29, 30, 31, 44
System CGI methods, 106, 107
system requirements, xiii

T

tab-delimited data, 52, 57
tab-separated text, 52
Table > Split Cell command, 57
table-based layouts, 45
Table button, 46
Table dialog, 46, 57

\<table\> tag, 55, 57

tables, 45–57

    adding rows/columns to, 47, 48, 49, 51

    adding to Web pages, 46–47

    aligning text in, 50–51

    and compound styles, 96

    creating layouts with, 45

    default settings for, 57

    importing data into, 52–54, 57

    inserting images into, 57

    labeling cells in, 46, 47, 50

    merging cells in, 50

    previewing in Web browsers, 51, 54

    saving, 47, 51

    selecting cells in, 48

    setting width of, 46

    sorting, 55–56, 57

    splitting cells in, 57

    zooming in on, 49

tabular data

    importing, 52–54, 57

    sorting, 55–56, 57

tag-based styles, 77, 84–85

Tag Inspector tab, 96

Target menu, Properties panel, 26, 62

Target Rule menu, Properties panel, 80

\<td\> tag, 48

text

    adding to Web page, 15–16

    flowing around images, 42–43

    formatting, 15

    size considerations, 24

    starting new paragraphs, 15

text color, 85, 88, 90, 93, 101

Text-decoration checkbox, 72, 74

Text Field button, Forms tab, 107

text links, 60–62, 75

Textarea button, Forms tab, 108

thumbnails

    creating, 37–39

    renaming, 39

    zooming in/out on, 7

titles, page, 12, 13, 24

toolbars

    Document. See Document toolbar

    Insert. See Insert toolbar

    Related Files, 13

    showing/hiding, 3

    Standard, 2

Toolbars command, 3

\<tr\> tag, 48

Trash can, 82

two-column liquid layouts, 12, 87

Type category, CSS Rule Definition dialog, 85, 88, 90, 93

U

Undo Crop command, 34

Unordered List button, 22

unvisited links, 70

uploading

    multiple files, 130–131, 133

    single page, 132

V

Value window, Properties panel, 111

versiontracker.com, 25

Vert pop-up menu, 50

vertical alignment, in tables, 50

Vertical button, Spry Menu Bar, 112

video files

    Flash, 29–31

    QuickTime, 32

View > Split Vertically command, 2

index

View > Toolbars command, 3
view setups, 7
visited links, 70, 74
Visual Aids, 75
Visual QuickProject Guides, vii, x–xi
Visual QuickStart Guides, xiv, 77
visually impaired visitors, 44, 57

W

waywest.net, xii
Web browsers
    audio, 44, 46, 57
    checking remote site pages in, 131
    and liquid layouts, 12
    previewing menus in, 102, 105
    previewing tables in, 51, 54
    testing links in, 61
Web-crawler programs, 63, 106
Web-hosting firms, 128, 133
Web pages. See also home page; Web site(s)
    adding footers to, 23
    adding images to, 27–28
    adding interactivity to. See interactivity
    adding jump menus to, 103–105
    adding navigation menus to, 3, 98–102
    adding search terms to, 122–123, 133
    adding tables to, 46–47
    adding text to, 15–16
    adding video to, 29–33
    allowing visitors to jump to specific spot in, 64–65
    attaching/detaching styles sheets for, 82–83
    creating headings for, 19–20, 24

    dragging images from Bridge to, 7
    formatting. See style sheets
    importing tabular data into, 52–54
    inserting image placeholders in, 17–18
    inserting library items in, 119
    linking, 59, 60–62. See also links
    naming, 24
    natural flow for, 83
    publishing, 121, 130–132
    using style sheets for. See style sheets
Web Premium edition, CS4, xiii
Web search engines, 122
Web site(s). See also Web pages
    adding interactivity to. See interactivity
    checking/fixing links in, 124
    collecting information from visitors to, 106–111
    creating basic, 11–24
    creating home page for, 12–14
    creating links between pages on, 60–61
    helping search engines find, 122–123
    naming, 8, 10
    publishing, 121, 130–132
    setting up local version of, 8–9, 10
    this book's companion, vii, xii
    tools for creating, vii, xiii
Web Standard edition, CS4, xiii
widgets, Spry, 3, 98
Window > Assets command, 114, 115
Window > CSS Styles command, 78
Window > Insert command, 3
Windows systems, text size on, 24
workspaces, 4, 10, 27, 29
wrapping text, 42

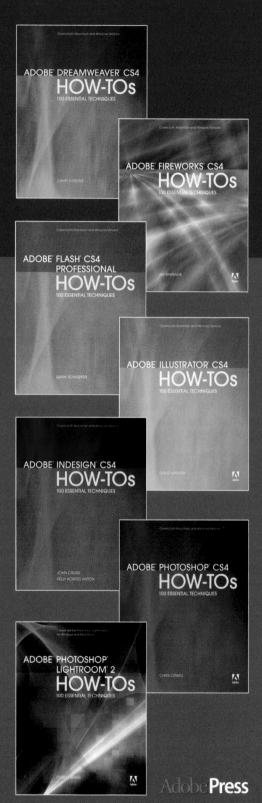

GET UP AND RUNNING QUICKLY!

For more than 15 years, the practical approach to the best-selling *Visual QuickStart Guide* series from Peachpit Press has helped millions of readers—from developers to designers to systems administrators and more—get up to speed on all sorts of computer programs. Now with select titles in full color, *Visual QuickStart Guide* books provide an even easier and more enjoyable way for readers to learn about new technology through task-based instruction, friendly prose, and visual explanations.

Task-Based
Information is broken down into concise, one- and two-page tasks to help you get right to work.

Visual
Hundreds of screen shots illustrate the steps and show you the best way to do them.

Step by Step
Numbered, easy-to-follow instructions guide you through each task.

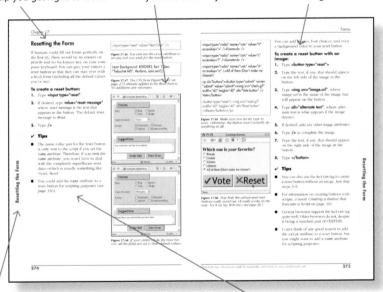

Quick Reference
Tabs on each page identify the task, making it easy to find what you're looking for.

Tips
Lots of helpful tips are featured throughout the book.